The Tragedy of
JULIUS CAESAR

with Related Readings

SERIES EDITORS

Dom Saliani   **Chris Ferguson**   **Dr. Tim Scott**

I(T)P *International Thomson Publishing*

Albany • Bonn • Boston • Cincinnati • Detroit • London • Madrid • Melbourne • Mexico City •
New York • Pacific Grove • Paris • San Francisco • Singapore • Tokyo • Toronto • Washington

International Thomson Publishing, 1997

Published simultaneously in 1997 by International Thomson Limited:

ITP Nelson (Canada)   **South-Western Educational Publishing (U.S.A.)**
Nelson ITP (Australia)   **Thomas Nelson United Kingdom**

ISBN 0-17-606615-2

Cataloguing in Publication Data

Shakespeare, William, 1564-1616
     [Julius Caesar]
   The tragedy of Julius Caesar with related readings

(The global Shakespeare series)
ISBN 0-17-606615-2

1. Shakespeare, William, 1564-1616.   Julius
Caesar.   I. Title.   II. Series.

PR2808.A1   1997   822.3'3   C97-930212-9

Acquisitions Editor: TARA STEELE
Project Managers: JAN HARKNESS (CANADA)
                   JACKIE TIDEY (AUSTRALIA)
                   LAURIE WENDELL (U.S.A.)
Series Designer: LIZ HARASYMCZUK
Cover Illustrator: YUAN LEE
Production Editors: KAREN ALLISTON, KATHLEEN FFOLLIOTT,
                   SANDRA MANLEY
Sr. Composition Analyst: DARYN DEWALT
Production Coordinator: DONNA BROWN
Permissions Editor: VICKI GOULD
Research: LISA BRANT
Film: IMAGING EXCELLENCE

Printed and bound in Canada
 2 3 4 5 ML 01 00 99 98

Contents

Features of the *Global Shakespeare Series*

Introduction to the Play: Information on the date, sources, themes, and appeal of the play, notes on Shakespeare's use of verse and prose, and common stage directions all help to set a context for the play.

The Text: The *Global Shakespeare Series* is faithful to Shakespeare's full original texts. Spelling and punctuation have been modernized to make the plays accessible to today's readers. For the last 200 years, many editors have chosen to arrange and rearrange Shakespeare's words to create a consistent iambic pentameter in the text. For example, a dialogue involving short speeches would look like this:

CASSIUS: Who's there?
CASCA: A Roman.
CASSIUS: Casca by your voice.

Together the three lines make up 10 syllables. In some cases, editors have even taken words from one line and combined them with words from another line to create the iambic pentameter pattern. Shakespeare did not do this in his original text. The *Global Shakespeare Series* has not adopted this convention. What you see is what Shakespeare wrote.

Dramatis Personae: The list of characters is organized by families or by loyalty affiliations.

Scene Summaries: Brief synopses help you to follow and anticipate developments in the plot.

Artwork and Graphics: Original artwork has been created and designed for this series by internationally acclaimed artists.

Marginal Notes: Generous notes define difficult or archaic vocabulary. In some cases, entire sentences of Shakespeare are paraphrased into modern idiom — these are identified with quotation marks.

Notes of Interest: Longer notes provide background information on Shakespeare's times or interesting interpretations of various speeches or characters.

Quotable Notables: Brief comments on various aspects of the play by authors, celebrities, and highly regarded literary critics and professors are included. The views do not necessarily reflect the views of the editors; they are merely springboards for discussion, debate, and reflection.

Related Reading References: These references indicate that there is a piece of literature in the latter part of the book that relates well to a specific scene or speech.

Considerations: Each Act is followed by a series of scene-specific "considerations." Some involve analysis and interpretation; others will offer opportunities to be creative and imaginative.

Related Readings: The second half of the text contains poems, short stories, short drama, and non-fiction pieces that are directly related to the play. These can be read for enjoyment or for enrichment. They emphasize the continuing relevance of Shakespeare in today's society.

The 10 Most Challenging Questions: These questions are ideal for developing into research or independent study projects.

Introduction to *Julius Caesar*

Appeal of *Julius Caesar*

Julius Caesar is one of Shakespeare's best-known tragedies. For over 400 years, readers and theatre audiences all over the world have been moved by the grandeur and scope of this story, taken directly from the annals of Roman history. It continues to be one of Shakespeare's most often performed plays.

Why do people never tire of *Julius Caesar*? Perhaps its lasting appeal can be attributed to the play's unforgettable characters, gripping plot, revelations of human nature, universal themes, and lyrical poetry.

Julius Caesar is Shakespeare's only play that deals with a historical figure of the highest magnitude. Hamlet, Macbeth, and King Lear are but minor historical figures compared to the place Julius Caesar holds in history. Elizabethan audiences were fascinated with the personage of Caesar, as are modern audiences.

A Problem Play

In addition to *Julius Caesar's* appeal as a great story taken from a chapter in history, the play is also an intriguing puzzle. It poses a number of problems in that it is not entirely clear who the central character is. Some scholars even argue that the play is misnamed because the real focus of the tragedy is on Brutus rather than Caesar. Others counter that it is Caesar and Caesar's spirit that dominate the action, and therefore it is his tragedy that unifies the play. Still others suggest that the real hero of the play is Rome itself, and the tragedy revolves around Rome's inability to remain free of tyranny and civil strife. The play supports all of these views and others.

Caesar—Hero or Tyrant?

Although it is not clear to modern audiences who the hero and villain(s) are in this tragedy, there would have been less confusion for the Elizabethan audiences. They would have seen Caesar as Rome's legitimate ruler and his murder as a violation of the "natural order." Furthermore, most modern audiences perceive Caesar as being pompous and overly proud. The Elizabethans, however, would have seen things quite differently. Caesar's speech and deportment were what they would have expected from someone who was, in Brutus' words, "the foremost man of all the world."

The assassination of Caesar was considered for many hundreds of years to be one of the vilest crimes of all time. The Italian medieval poet Dante (1265–1321), in "Inferno,"—Part 1 of his *Divine Comedy* — went so far as to place Brutus beside Judas Iscariot in the seventh and lowest circle of Hell. Shakespeare himself refers to the murder in *The Second Part of Henry the Sixth*, in which he provides a list of "great men" who have died at the hands of "vile besonians" (beggars). He writes that "... Brutus' bastard hand/Stabbed Julius Caesar" (Act Four, Scene 1).

American Revolutionists interpreted the play quite differently. They saw it as condemning tyranny and defending the freedom made possible by a republican form of government. They went so far as to use lines from the play as rallying cries. Patrick Henry's "Give me liberty or give me death" owes its origin to Cassius' outcry in Act Three, Scene 1. Modern interpretations attempt to make the play more relevant by drawing parallels between Caesar and dictators such as Hitler and Mussolini.

Can this question of hero or tyrant be satisfactorily answered? Perhaps one reason for the play's continuing appeal is that the issue is not an easy one to resolve.

Interpreting Shakespeare

It was not uncommon in Shakespeare's day to have characters explain themselves directly to the audience either in a soliloquy or through dialogue.

This outdated dramatic technique is not very realistic, but it was helpful in clarifying character and themes. When characters such as Caesar and Brutus speak highly of themselves, modern audiences interpret their speeches as evidence of vanity and boastfulness. This was not Shakespeare's intention. When Caesar declares that he is fearless, this is not a boast but rather a method of telling the audience that Caesar is without fear. Likewise, when Brutus emphasizes that he is noble and honest, we must be careful not to add "arrogant" to his list of self-declared traits.

There are occasions in the play, however, when the characters go beyond merely explaining themselves to the audience. The task of the careful reader is to determine when these occasions occur.

Historical Background

According to "historical legend," Rome was established in 753 B.C.E. For two hundred years, it was ruled by a series of tyrant kings, the Tarquins, who were overthrown in 510 B.C.E. due to the efforts of Lucius Junius Brutus, an ancestor of the Brutus in this play. A democratic republic was formed that lasted for almost five hundred years—until the time of Caesar's death. The Romans were extremely proud of their democratic traditions. For them, the thought of being ruled by a king was repugnant.

Gaius Julius Caesar was born in 100 B.C.E. He gained power and wealth through a series of successful military campaigns in which he conquered Britain, Gaul (France), much of Central and Eastern Europe, and parts of North Africa. His famous utterance "*Veni, vidi, vici*" (I came, I saw, I conquered) is apt.

Caesar was interested in much more than just military conquest. After a series of civil wars that lasted until 48 B.C.E., Caesar had himself declared Rome's dictator for life. He was a popular politician and served well as Rome's supreme leader. He built roads, developed irrigation systems, and financed public parks and buildings. He even reformed the calendar. However, it was clear to most people that Caesar wanted more than just power. He also wanted a title worthy of his stature. By 44 B.C.E., he was ready to declare himself King of Rome and do away with the five-century-old republic.

THE TRAGEDIE OF
IVLIVS CÆSAR.

Actus Primus. Scœna Prima.

Enter Flauius, Murellus, and certaine Commoners ouer the Stage.

Flauius.

HEnce: home you idle Creatures, get you home:
Is this a Holiday? What, know you not
(Being Mechanicall) you ought not walke
Vpon a labouring day, without the signe
Of your Profession? Speake, what Trade art thou?

Car. Why Sir, a Carpenter.

Mur. Where is thy Leather Apron, and thy Rule?
What dost thou with thy best Apparrell on?
You sir, what Trade are you?

Cobl. Truly Sir, in respect of a fine Workman, I am but as you would say, a Cobler.

Mur. But what Trade art thou? Answer me directly.

Cob. A Trade Sir, that I hope I may vse, with a safe Conscience, which is indeed Sir, a Mender of bad soules.

Fla. What Trade thou knaue? Thou naughty knaue, what Trade?

Cobl. Nay I beseech you Sir, be not out with me: yet if you be out Sir, I can mend you.

Mur. What mean'st thou by that? Mend mee, thou sawcy Fellow?

Cob. Why sir, Cobble you.

Fla. Thou art a Cobler, art thou?

Cob. Truly sir, all that I liue by, is with the Aule: I meddle with no Tradesmans matters, nor womens matters; but withall I am indeed Sir, a Surgeon to old shooes: when they are in great danger, I recouer them. As proper men as euer trod vpon Neats Leather, haue gone vpon my handy-worke.

Fla. But wherefore art not in thy Shop to day?
Why do'st thou leade these men about the streets?

Cob. Truly sir, to weare out their shooes, to get my selfe into more worke. But indeede sir, we make Holyday to see Cæsar, and to reioyce in his Triumph.

Mur. Wherefore reioyce?
What Conquest brings he home?
What Tributaries follow him to Rome,
To grace in Captiue bonds his Chariot Wheeles?
You Blockes, you stones, you worse then senslesse things:
O you hard hearts, you cruell men of Rome,
Knew you not Pompey many a time and oft?
Haue you climb'd vp to Walles and Battlements,
To Towres and Windowes? Yea, to Chimney tops,
Your Infants in your Armes, and there haue sate
The liue-long day, with patient expectation,

To see great Pompey passe the streets of Rome:
And when you saw his Chariot but appeare,
Haue you not made an Vniuersall shout,
That Tyber trembled vnderneath her bankes
To heare the replication of your sounds,
Made in her Concaue Shores?
And do you now put on your best attyre?
And do you now cull out a Holy day?
And do you now strew Flowers in his way,
That comes in Triumph ouer Pompeyes blood?
Be gone,
Runne to your houses, fall vpon your knees,
Pray to the Gods to intermit the plague
That needs must light on this Ingratitude.

Fla. Go, go, good Countrymen, and for this fault
Assemble all the poore men of your sort;
Draw them to Tyber bankes, and weepe your teares
Into the Channell, till the lowest streame
Do kisse the most exalted Shores of all.

Exeunt all the Commoners.

See where their basest mettle be not mou'd,
They vanish tongue-tyed in their guiltinesse:
Go you downe that way towards the Capitoll,
This way will I: Disrobe the Images,
If you do finde them deckt with Ceremonies.

Mur. May we do so?
You know it is the Feast of Lupercall.

Fla. It is no matter, let no Images
Be hung with Cæsars Trophees: Ile about,
And driue away the Vulgar from the streets;
So do you too, where you perceiue them thicke.
These growing Feathers, pluckt from Cæsars wing,
Will make him flye an ordinary pitch,
Who else would soare aboue the view of men,
And keepe vs all in seruile fearefulnesse. *Exeunt*

*Enter Cæsar, Antony for the Course, Calphurnia, Portia, De-
cius, Cicero, Brutus, Cassius, Caska, a Soothsayer: after them Murellus and Flauius.*

Cæs. Calphurnia.

Cask. Peace ho, Cæsar speakes.

Cæs. Calphurnia.

Calp. Heere my Lord.

Cæs. Stand you directly in Antonio's way,
When he doth run his course. Antonio.

Ant. Cæsar, my Lord.

Cæs. Forget not in your speed Antonio,
To touch Calphurnia: for our Elders say,

k k

The

First page of *Julius Caesar* from the First Folio, 1623

Introduction to *Julius Caesar*

Sources and Date of the Play

"Not that it matters, but most of what follows is true." So begins the 1972 classic film *Butch Cassidy and the Sundance Kid*. The same comment can also be made about *Julius Caesar*. Shakespeare's primary source for the play was Plutarch's *The Lives of the Noble Grecians and Romans*, first translated into English by Thomas North in 1579.

Shakespeare derived much of his information from three separate chapters in North's translation, and he remained quite faithful to the source. In fact, as many critics have noted, in some places Shakespeare lifted entire passages of North's prose and used almost every word in transforming them to verse. But Shakespeare also intro-

duced much that is not in Plutarch's work. The funeral orations, for example, are Shakespeare's, as are the portrayals of many of the minor characters.

In 1623, thirty-six of Shakespeare's plays were collected together and printed in a volume now referred to as the First Folio. It is in this collection that *The Tragedy of Julius Caesar* first appeared. Of note is the fact that Julius Caesar is the most accurately printed play in the Folio. Greater care was taken in editing this play than any other in the collection.

Scholars are divided as to when the play was actually written. Some place the composition date as early as 1591 and others as late as 1596. We have an eyewitness account of a performance of the play on September 21, 1599. This would have made it one of the first plays performed at the newly built Globe Theatre.

A performance at the Globe Theatre

Shakespeare's Verse and Prose

Many students find Shakespeare difficult to read and understand. They often ask whether or not the Elizabethans really spoke the way Shakespeare's characters do. The answer is, of course, no. Shakespeare wrote using a poetic form known as *blank verse*. This produces an elevated style of speech that would have been very different from everyday speech during the Elizabethan period.

Furthermore, the blank verse contains a rhythm pattern known as *iambic pentameter*. What this means is that most lines contain five feet (pentameter) and each foot contains an unstressed and a stressed syllable (an iamb). In other words, as Shakespeare wrote, playing in the back of his mind was a rhythm pattern that would sound like:

da DA da DA da DA da DA da DA

Caesar's famous self-declaration in Act Three would look like this in terms of stressed and unstressed syllables:

~ / ~ / ~ / ~ / ~ /
But I am constant as the Northern Star

Julius Caesar is approximately 2700 lines long, and of these, 300 are written in prose. Prose contrasts strongly with the elevated style of blank verse. Persons of noble birth speak in verse and servants and members of the lower classes usually speak in prose. When the noble Brutus speaks with others in his own class, he uses verse. However, when he addresses the commoners at Caesar's funeral, he uses prose. Letters and documents, scenes of comic relief, and scenes involving madness are also usually written in prose.

The Text and Stage Directions

The edition for this text is faithful to the 1623 First Folio. Spelling and punctuation have been modernized to make the reading more accessible to today's readers.

Shakespeare used stage directions very sparingly in his plays. Because he was directly involved in the production of the plays, there was little need for him to record the stage directions.

In this edition, the stage directions that appear in italics are Shakespeare's. Directions that are included in square brackets [ ] have been added by the editor. A long dash "—" in a speech indicates that the speaker is addressing someone other than the person to whom the actor was first speaking.

The following stage directions appear frequently in Shakespeare's plays:

Above, aloft – scene played in the balcony above the stage level or from higher up in the loft
Alarum – a loud shout, a signal call to arms
Aside – spoken directly to the audience and not heard by the others on the stage
Below, beneath – speech or scene played from below the surface of the stage. The actor stands inside an open trap-door.
Exit – he/she leaves the stage
Exeunt – they leave the stage
Flourish – fanfare of trumpets; usually announces the entrance of royalty
Hautboys – musicians enter, playing wind instruments
Omnes – all; everyone
Torchbearers – actors carry torches, a clue to the audience that the scene takes place in the dark, either at night or in an area that is not naturally lit
Within – words spoken off-stage in what the audience would assume is an unseen room, corridor, or the outdoors

The Roman Republic in the time of
JULIUS CAESAR

Nervii

GAUL

Rubicon R.

Tiber R.

SPAIN

Rome

ITALY

Philippi

Sardis

Mediterranean Sea

N

ROMAN REPUBLIC

Dramatis Personae

Household of Caesar:

JULIUS CAESAR
CALPURNIA Wife to Caesar

Leaders of Rome after the death of Julius Caesar:

OCTAVIUS CAESAR Nephew to Julius Caesar
MARCUS ANTONIUS
LEPIDUS

Household of Brutus:

MARCUS BRUTUS Leader of the conspirators
PORTIA Wife to Brutus
LUCIUS Servant

Conspirators:

CASSIUS
CASCA
CINNA
TREBONIUS
LIGARIUS
DECIUS BRUTUS
METELLUS CIMBER

Senators:

CICERO
POPILIUS LENA
PUBLIUS

Tribunes:

FLAVIUS
MARULLUS

Officers and Soldiers in the Armies of Brutus and Cassius:

CLITUS
CLAUDIO
DARDANIUS
LUCILIUS
MESSALA
STRATO
TITINIUS
VARRUS
VOLUMNIUS
YOUNG CATO

Others of Rome and elsewhere:

ARTEMIDORUS Teacher of rhetoric
A SOOTHSAYER
CINNA A poet
ANOTHER POET In Brutus' camp
PINDARUS Slave to Cassius
A COBBLER
A CARPENTER

Other Senators, Plebeians, Guards, Attendants, Messengers, etc.

Scene: Rome, Sardis, Philippi

Act One
Scene 1

Rome. A street.

It is February 15, 44 B.C.E. Two tribunes, Flavius and Marullus, encounter a group of tradesmen celebrating Caesar's victory over Pompey's forces. The tribunes shame the workers by reminding them of how they used to rejoice at Pompey's triumphs.

Enter Flavius, Marullus, and certain Commoners.

FLAVIUS: Hence, home you idle creatures, get you home!
    Is this a holiday? What, know you not,
    Being mechanical, you ought not walk
    Upon a labouring day without the sign
    Of your profession? Speak, what trade art thou?
CARPENTER: Why, sir, a carpenter.
MARULLUS: Where is thy leather apron and thy rule?
    What dost thou with thy best apparel on?
    You sir, what trade are you?
COBBLER: Truly sir, in respect of a fine workman, I am   10
    but, as you would say, a cobbler.
MARULLUS: But what trade art thou? Answer me directly.
COBBLER: A trade, sir, that I hope I may use with a safe
    conscience, which is, indeed sir, a mender of bad soles.
MARULLUS: What trade, thou knave? Thou naughty knave,
    what trade?
COBBLER: Nay I beseech you sir, be not out with me. Yet,
    if you be out, sir, I can mend you.
MARULLUS: What meanest thou by that? Mend me, thou
    saucy fellow!   20
COBBLER: Why sir, cobble you.
FLAVIUS: Thou art a cobbler, art thou?
COBBLER: Truly sir, all that I live by, is with the awl. I
    meddle with no tradesman's matters, nor women's
    matters, but withal I am, indeed, sir, a surgeon to old
    shoes. When they are in great danger, I recover them. As
    proper men as ever trod upon neat's leather, have gone
    upon my handiwork.

RELATED READING

Historical Background to Julius Caesar – historical essay by Isaac Asimov (page 115)

3. *mechanical* – of the working class
11. *cobbler* – wordplay; a mender of shoes or a bungler

The puns and details in this scene with the *mechanicals* would have appealed directly to the groundlings in Shakespeare's day. The details about daily life come from Elizabethan England and not from Rome.

18. *be out* – wordplay; angry or in need of a shoe repair
23. *awl* – shoemaker's tool

awl

25. *withal* – wordplay; "with awl"
27. *neat's leather* - cowhide

FLAVIUS: But wherefore art not in thy shop today?
   Why dost thou lead these men about the streets?   30
COBBLER: Truly, sir, to wear out their shoes, to get myself
   into more work. But, indeed, sir, we make holiday, to see
   Caesar and to rejoice in his triumph.
MARULLUS: Wherefore rejoice?
   What conquest brings he home?
   What tributaries follow him to Rome,
   To grace in captive bonds his chariot wheels?
   You blocks, you stones, you worse than senseless things!
   O you hard hearts, you cruel men of Rome,
   Knew you not Pompey? Many a time and oft   40
   Have you climbed up to walls and battlements,
   To towers and windows, yea, to chimney-tops,
   Your infants in your arms, and there have sat
   The livelong day, with patient expectation,
   To see great Pompey pass the streets of Rome.
   And when you saw his chariot but appear,
   Have you not made an universal shout,
   That Tiber trembled underneath her banks,
   To hear the replication of your sounds
   Made in her concave shores?   50
   And do you now put on your best attire?
   And do you now cull out a holiday?
   And do you now strew flowers in his way,
   That comes in triumph over Pompey's blood?
   Be gone!
   Run to your houses, fall upon your knees,
   Pray to the gods to intermit the plague
   That needs must light on this ingratitude.
FLAVIUS: Go, go, good countrymen, and, for this fault,
   Assemble all the poor men of your sort,   60
   Draw them to Tiber banks, and weep your tears
   Into the channel, till the lowest stream
   Do kiss the most exalted shores of all.

Exeunt all the Commoners.

See whether their basest metal be not moved.
They vanish tongue-tied in their guiltiness.
Go you down that way towards the Capitol.
This way will I. Disrobe the images,
If you do find them decked with ceremonies.

MARULLUS: May we do so?
    You know it is the Feast of Lupercal.   70
FLAVIUS: It is no matter. Let no images
    Be hung with Caesar's trophies. I'll about,
    And drive away the vulgar from the streets.
    So do you too, where you perceive them thick.
    These growing feathers plucked from Caesar's wing
    Will make him fly an ordinary pitch,
    Who else would soar above the view of men,
    And keep us all in servile fearfulness.

Exeunt.

70. *Feast of Lupercal* – a spring fertility festival celebrated on February 15. It would be considered a sacrilege to rip down decorations put up to celebrate the Pan-like god Lupercus.

73. *vulgar* – Today this term has negative connotations, but such was not the case in Shakespeare's or Caesar's day. In Latin, the word *vulgus* means simply "common people."

76. *pitch* – height

77. *else* – otherwise

77 – 78. Flavius expresses what is to be a recurrent theme in the play: Romans, proud of their republican traditions, fear that Caesar will soar so high that he will become all-powerful, like a god, and that Romans will consequently lose their cherished freedom.

Act One
Scene 2

Rome. A public place.

Enter Caesar, Antony for the course, Calpurnia, Portia, Decius, Cicero, Brutus, Cassius, Casca, a Soothsayer; after them Marullus and Flavius.

CAESAR: Calpurnia!
CASCA: Peace ho! Caesar speaks.
CAESAR: Calpurnia!
CALPURNIA: Here my lord.
CAESAR: Stand you directly in Antonio's way
  When he doth run his course. Antonio.
ANTONY: Caesar, my lord?
CAESAR: Forget not, in your speed, Antonio,
  To touch Calpurnia; for our elders say,
  The barren touched in this holy chase,   10
  Shake off their sterile curse.
ANTONY: I shall remember.
  When Caesar says, "Do this," it is performed.
CAESAR: Set on, and leave no ceremony out.
SOOTHSAYER: Caesar!
CAESAR: Ha! Who calls?
CASCA: Bid every noise be still. Peace yet again.
CAESAR: Who is it in the press, that calls on me?
  I hear a tongue, shriller than all the music
  Cry, "Caesar!" Speak. Caesar is turned to hear.   20
SOOTHSAYER: Beware the ides of March.
CAESAR: What man is that?
BRUTUS: A soothsayer bids you beware the ides of March.
CAESAR: Set him before me. Let me see his face.
CASSIUS: Fellow, come from the throng. Look upon Caesar.

Caesar's first words reveal that he has a superstitious nature. As part of the Lupercalian ritual, he would like his wife Calpurnia to be touched by Antony and thereby cured of her sterility. When Caesar is warned by a Soothsayer to beware the ides of March, he dismisses the man as a dreamer. Cassius attempts to convince Brutus to join in a conspiracy against Caesar. Casca describes how Caesar was offered a crown three times. Brutus promises to think about what Cassius has said and to meet with him the next day.

6. *run his course* – Plutarch tells us that on the day of the feast "noblemen's sons, young men ... run naked through the city, striking in sport those they meet with leather thongs." It was believed that if women who could not bear children were touched by these men during the run, they would be cured of their sterility.

15. *Soothsayer* – one who can foretell the future
18. *press* – throng, crowd
21. *ides* – mid-point of the month; i.e., the fifteenth day

CAESAR: What sayest thou to me now? Speak once again.
SOOTHSAYER: Beware the ides of March.
CAESAR: He is a dreamer. Let us leave him. Pass.

Sennet. Exeunt all but Brutus and Cassius.

CASSIUS: Will you go see the order of the course?
BRUTUS: Not I.   30
CASSIUS: I pray you, do.
BRUTUS: I am not gamesome. I do lack some part
    Of that quick spirit that is in Antony.
    Let me not hinder Cassius your desires.
    I'll leave you.
CASSIUS: Brutus, I do observe you now of late.
    I have not from your eyes that gentleness
    And show of love as I was wont to have.
    You bear too stubborn and too strange a hand
    Over your friend, that loves you.   40
BRUTUS: Cassius,
    Be not deceived. If I have veiled my look,
    I turn the trouble of my countenance
    Merely upon myself. Vexed I am
    Of late, with passions of some difference,
    Conceptions only proper to my self,
    Which give some soil, perhaps, to my behaviours.
    But let not therefore my good friends be grieved
    (Among which number, Cassius, be you one)
    Nor construe any further my neglect,   50
    Than that poor Brutus with himself at war,
    Forgets the shows of love to other men.
CASSIUS: Then Brutus, I have much mistook your passion,
    By means whereof, this breast of mine hath buried
    Thoughts of great value, worthy cogitations.
    Tell me, good Brutus, can you see your face?
BRUTUS: No, Cassius;
    For the eye sees not itself but by reflection,
    By some other things.
CASSIUS: 'Tis just,   60
    And it is very much lamented Brutus,
    That you have no such mirrors as will turn
    Your hidden worthiness into your eye,
    That you might see your shadow.
    I have heard,
    Where many of the best respect in Rome,
    Except immortal Caesar, speaking of Brutus,

23. Note that Caesar does not initially hear the Soothsayer's words. It is Brutus who delivers the warning to Caesar.

29. *order ... course* – progress of the race

32. *gamesome* – wordplay; frivolous or fond of sports

38. *wont* – accustomed
39 – 40. "You appear stern and even hostile to your friend."
42. *veiled my look* – not been open
43. *countenance* – facial expression
45. *passions ... difference* – conflicting emotions
46. *Conceptions ... my self* – thoughts or ideas that are of concern to me alone
47. *soil* – blemish

48. Brutus was a follower of Stoicism, a philosophy that taught that the mind is more powerful than the body, that one should work to control emotions, ignore pain, and remain in control of one's state of mind. Mr. Spock, in the original *Star Trek* series, would have made a perfect Stoic.

54. *By means whereof* – and as a result
55. *worthy cogitations* – important considerations
64. *shadow* – reflection

68. *this age's yoke* – the oppression (loss of freedom) caused by Caesar's increasing power

"Poetry is a more philosophic and a finer thing than history, since poetry speaks of universals and history only of particulars."
– Aristotle (384 – 322 B.C.E.), Greek philosopher

77. *discover* – reveal
79. *jealous on* – suspicious of
80. *common laughter* – laughingstock
81. *stale* – cheapen
82. *protester* – one who professes (love or friendship)
86. *rout* – rabble, commoners
93. *wherefore* – why; for what purpose
95. *aught toward* – anything concerning
98. *speed me* – enable me to succeed
101. *outward favour* – external appearance
105. *had as lief* – would just as soon as
106. "In fear of a fellow human being such as myself."

111. *chafing with* – beating against; raging
113. *angry flood* – turbulent water
115. *Accoutred* – dressed
119. "And making progress with hearts aroused by the spirit of competition"
120. *ere* – before

And groaning underneath this age's yoke,
Have wished that noble Brutus had his eyes.
BRUTUS: Into what dangers would you   70
Lead me, Cassius,
That you would have me seek into myself
For that which is not in me?
CASSIUS: Therefore, good Brutus, be prepared to hear.
And since you know you cannot see yourself
So well as by reflection, I, your glass,
Will modestly discover to yourself
That of yourself which you yet know not of.
And be not jealous on me, gentle Brutus.
Were I a common laughter, or did use   80
To stale with ordinary oaths my love
To every new protester; if you know
That I do fawn on men, and hug them hard,
And after scandal them; or if you know
That I profess myself in banqueting
To all the rout, then hold me dangerous.

Flourish, and shout.

BRUTUS: What means this shouting?
I do fear, the people choose Caesar
For their king.
CASSIUS: Ay, do you fear it?   90
Then must I think you would not have it so.
BRUTUS: I would not Cassius, yet I love him well.
But wherefore do you hold me here so long?
What is it, that you would impart to me?
If it be aught toward the general good,
Set honour in one eye, and death in the other,
And I will look on both indifferently,
For let the gods so speed me, as I love
The name of honour, more than I fear death.
CASSIUS: I know that virtue to be in you, Brutus,   100
As well as I do know your outward favour.
Well, honour is the subject of my story.
I cannot tell, what you and other men
Think of this life, but, for my single self,
I had as lief not be as live to be
In awe of such a thing, as I myself.
I was born free as Caesar, so were you.
We both have fed as well, and we can both
Endure the winter's cold, as well as he.

For once, upon a raw and gusty day,   110
The troubled Tiber, chafing with her shores,
Caesar said to me, "Darest thou, Cassius, now
Leap in with me into this angry flood,
And swim to yonder point?" Upon the word,
Accoutred as I was, I plunged in,
And bade him follow; so indeed he did.
The torrent roared, and we did buffet it
With lusty sinews, throwing it aside
And stemming it with hearts of controversy.
But ere we could arrive the point proposed,   120
Caesar cried, "Help me, Cassius, or I sink."
I, as Aeneas, our great ancestor,
Did from the flames of Troy upon his shoulder
The old Anchises bear, so, from the waves of Tiber
Did I the tired Caesar. And this man,
Is now become a god, and Cassius is
A wretched creature, and must bend his body,
If Caesar carelessly but nod on him.
He had a fever when he was in Spain,
And when the fit was on him, I did mark   130
How he did shake. 'Tis true, this god did shake.
His coward lips did from their colour fly,
And that same eye, whose bend doth awe the world
Did lose his lustre. I did hear him groan,
Ay, and that tongue of his, that bade the Romans
Mark him, and write his speeches in their books,
Alas, it cried, "Give me some drink Titinius,"
As a sick girl. Ye gods, it doth amaze me,
A man of such a feeble temper should
So get the start of the majestic world   140
And bear the palm alone.

Shout. Flourish.

Brutus: Another general shout?
    I do believe that these applauses are
    For some new honours that are heaped on Caesar.
Cassius: Why man, he doth bestride the narrow world
    Like a Colossus, and we petty men
    Walk under his huge legs, and peep about
    To find ourselves dishonourable graves.
    Men at some time are masters of their fates.
    The fault, dear Brutus, is not in our stars,   150
    But in ourselves, that we are underlings.

Sidebar notes:

122 – 124. *Aeneas ... Anchises* – The Romans traced their ancestry back to Aeneas, a Prince of Troy. In Homer's *Iliad* and Virgil's *Aeneid,* we learn that after ten long years of war the Greeks defeated the Trojans and sacked their city. Aeneas carried his father, Anchises, through the flames of Troy and fled the city with a group of followers. Aeneas and his band eventually landed in Italy and founded the city of Rome.

127. *bend his body* – bow; show obedience
132. *from their colour fly* – turn pale
136. *Mark ... write* – pay close attention to and record
140. "So take the lead ahead of all others in this wide world"
141. *palm* – symbol of victory
146. *Colossus* – an allusion to the Colossus of Rhodes, one of the Seven Wonders of the World.

Colossus

150 – 151. *The fault ... ourselves* – Cassius adhered to the Epicurean philosophy which rejected the view that the gods or the planets influenced the fate of individuals. He argues that if we are oppressed or ruled over by one such as Caesar, we have only ourselves to blame.

19

Act One • Scene 2

156. *Conjure* – use them to call up spirits

160. *Age* – people of today
163. *famed with* – made famous by
165. *encompassed* – contained; had room for

166. *Rome ... room* – During the Elizabethan period, the words *Rome* and *room* were pronounced alike. Hence this line contains a wordplay.

169. *There ... Brutus* – In 510 B.C.E., Lucius Junius Brutus was instrumental in driving the Tarquin kings out of Rome and establishing the Roman Republic.
169. *brooked* – tolerated
172. *am ... jealous* – have no doubt
173. *aim* – idea
180. *meet* – appropriate; fitting

192. *sour* – bitter, cynical

"Brutus" and "Caesar." What should be in that "Caesar"?
Why should that name be sounded more than yours?
Write them together, yours is as fair a name.
Sound them, it doth become the mouth as well.
Weigh them, it is as heavy. Conjure with 'em,
"Brutus" will start a spirit as soon as "Caesar."
Now in the names of all the gods at once,
Upon what meat doth this our Caesar feed,
That he is grown so great? Age, thou art shamed.   160
Rome, thou hast lost the breed of noble bloods.
When went there by an age, since the great flood,
But it was famed with more than with one man?
When could they say, till now, that talked of Rome,
That her wide walks encompassed but one man?
Now is it Rome indeed and room enough
When there is in it but one only man.
O, you and I, have heard our fathers say,
There was a Brutus once, that would have brooked
The eternal devil to keep his state in Rome   170
As easily as a king.

BRUTUS: That you do love me, I am nothing jealous;
What you would work me to, I have some aim.
How I have thought of this and of these times,
I shall recount hereafter. For this present,
I would not so, with love I might entreat you,
Be any further moved. What you have said,
I will consider. What you have to say
I will with patience hear, and find a time
Both meet to hear and answer such high things.   180
Till then, my noble friend, chew upon this:
Brutus had rather be a villager
Than to repute himself a son of Rome
Under these hard conditions as this time
Is like to lay upon us.

CASSIUS: I am glad that my weak words
Have struck but thus much show of fire from Brutus.

Enter Caesar and his Train.

BRUTUS: The games are done,
And Caesar is returning.

CASSIUS: As they pass by,   190
Pluck Casca by the sleeve,
And he will, after his sour fashion, tell you
What hath proceeded worthy note today.

BRUTUS: I will do so. But look you Cassius,
The angry spot doth glow on Caesar's brow,
And all the rest look like a chidden train.
Calpurnia's cheek is pale, and Cicero
Looks with such ferret and such fiery eyes
As we have seen him in the Capitol
Being crossed in conference by some senators.   200

CASSIUS: Casca will tell us what the matter is.

CAESAR: Antonio.

ANTONY: Caesar?

CAESAR: Let me have men about me that are fat,
Sleek-headed men and such as sleep a-nights.
Yond Cassius has a lean and hungry look.
He thinks too much. Such men are dangerous.

ANTONY: Fear him not, Caesar, he's not dangerous.
He is a noble Roman, and well given.

CAESAR: Would he were fatter! But I fear him not.   210
Yet if my name were liable to fear,
I do not know the man I should avoid
So soon as that spare Cassius. He reads much,
He is a great observer, and he looks
Quite through the deeds of men. He loves no plays,
As thou dost, Antony; he hears no music;
Seldom he smiles, and smiles in such a sort
As if he mocked himself and scorned his spirit
That could be moved to smile at any thing.
Such men as he, be never at heart's ease,   220
Whiles they behold a greater than themselves,
And therefore are they very dangerous.
I rather tell thee what is to be feared,
Than what I fear. For always I am Caesar.
Come on my right hand, for this ear is deaf,
And tell me truly, what thou think'st of him.

Sennet. Exeunt Caesar and his Train.

CASCA: You pulled me by the cloak. Would you speak with
me?

BRUTUS: Ay, Casca. Tell us what hath chanced today
That Caesar looks so sad.   230

CASCA: Why you were with him, were you not?

BRUTUS: I should not then ask Casca what had chanced.

CASCA: Why there was a crown offered him; and being
offered him, he put it by with the back of his hand
thus, and then the people fell a-shouting.

196. *chidden* – scolded; chastised

197. *Cicero* – prominent orator and senator who was frequently at odds with Caesar and Mark Antony

200. *crossed in conference* – contradicted in a debate

205. *Sleek-headed* – well-groomed

209. *well given* – of good character

214 – 215. *looks ... men* – can see through men's actions and determine their motives

225. Notice that Caesar, having no sooner finished speaking of himself as being almost godlike, admits to an infirmity. Caesar's deafness is an invention of Shakespeare's. It is not mentioned at all in Plutarch.

BRUTUS: What was the second noise for?

CASCA: Why, for that too.

CASSIUS: They shouted thrice. What was the last cry for?

CASCA: Why, for that too.

BRUTUS: Was the crown offered him thrice?   240

CASCA: Ay, marry, was it, and he put it by thrice, every time gentler than other, and at every putting-by mine honest neighbours shouted.

CASSIUS: Who offered him the crown?

CASCA: Why, Antony.

BRUTUS: Tell us the manner of it, gentle Casca.

CASCA: I can as well be hanged as tell the manner of it. It was mere foolery. I did not mark it. I saw Mark Antony offer him a crown; yet 'twas not a crown neither, 'twas one of these coronets. And, as I told you, he put it   250
by once, but, for all that, to my thinking, he would fain have had it. Then he offered it to him again. Then he put it by again, but, to my thinking, he was very loath to lay his fingers off it. And then he offered it the third time. He put it the third time by, and still as he refused it, the rabblement hooted and clapped their chopt hands and threw up their sweaty night-caps, and uttered such a deal of stinking breath, because Caesar refused the crown that it had, almost choked Caesar, for he swounded and fell down at it. And for mine own part, I durst not laugh,   260
for fear of opening my lips, and receiving the bad air.

251. *fain* – gladly

256. *chopt* – chapped, rough

259. *swounded* – fainted

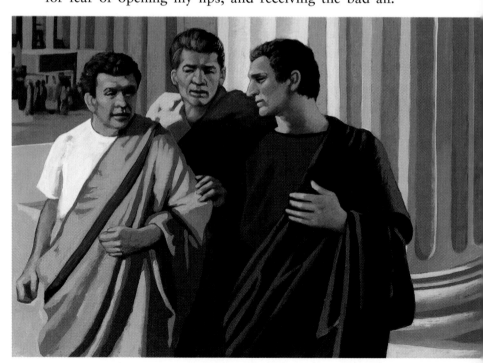

CASSIUS: But, soft, I pray you. What, did Caesar swound?

CASCA: He fell down in the market-place, and foamed at mouth, and was speechless.

BRUTUS: 'Tis very like he hath the falling sickness.

CASSIUS: No, Caesar hath it not. But you and I,
And honest Casca, we have the falling sickness.

CASCA: I know not what you mean by that, but I am sure Caesar fell down. If the tag-rag people did not clap him and hiss him, according as he pleased and displeased them, as they use to do the players in the theatre, I am no true man. 270

BRUTUS: What said he, when he came unto himself?

CASCA: Marry, before he fell down, when he perceived the common herd was glad he refused the crown, he plucked me ope his doublet and offered them his throat to cut. And I had been a man of any occupation, if I would not have taken him at a word, I would I might go to hell among the rogues. And so he fell. When he came to himself again, he said, if he had done or said anything amiss, he desired their worships to think it was his infirmity. Three or four wenches, where I stood, cried "Alas good soul," and forgave him with all their hearts. But there's no heed to be taken of them. If Caesar had stabbed their mothers, they would have done no less. 280

BRUTUS: And after that, he came thus sad, away?

CASCA: Ay.

267. *falling sickness* – epilepsy. Note that three lines later, Cassius turns this into a metaphor to describe the political situation as he sees it in Rome.

276. *doublet* – a tight-fitting jacket, popular during the Elizabethan period. In Shakespeare's day, actors did not wear period costumes. In other words, if a play were set in ancient Greece or Rome, the actors would still dress like Elizabethans. This convention did not change until David Garrick introduced the innovation of period costuming in the mid 1700s.

doublet

277 – 278. "If I had been one of them and of any trade, I would have taken him at his word and obeyed him."

CASSIUS: Did Cicero say anything?

CASCA: Ay, he spoke Greek.

CASSIUS: To what effect?   290

CASCA: Nay, and I tell you that, I'll never look you in the
face again. But those that understood him, smiled at one
another and shook their heads. But, for mine own part,
it was Greek to me. I could tell you more news too:
Marullus and Flavius, for pulling scarfs off Caesar's
images, are put to silence. Fare you well. There was more
foolery yet, if I could remember it.

CASSIUS: Will you sup with me tonight, Casca?

CASCA: No, I am promised forth.

CASSIUS: Will you dine with me tomorrow?   300

CASCA: Ay, if I be alive, and your mind hold and your dinner
worth the eating.

CASSIUS: Good. I will expect you.

CASCA: Do so. Farewell, both.

Exit [Casca].

BRUTUS: What a blunt fellow is this grown to be!
He was quick mettle when he went to school.

CASSIUS: So is he now, in execution
Of any bold, or noble enterprise,
However he puts on this tardy form.
This rudeness is a sauce to his good wit,   310
Which gives men stomach to digest his words
With better appetite.

BRUTUS: And so it is.
For this time I will leave you.
Tomorrow, if you please to speak with me,
I will come home to you, or if you will,
Come home to me, and I will wait for you.

CASSIUS: I will do so. Till then, think of the world.

Exit Brutus.

Well, Brutus, thou art noble. Yet, I see,
Thy honourable metal may be wrought   320
From that it is disposed. Therefore it is meet,
That noble minds keep ever with their likes,
For who so firm that cannot be seduced?
Caesar doth bear me hard, but he loves Brutus.
If I were Brutus now, and he were Cassius,
He should not humour me. I will this night,

291. *and* – if

296. *put to silence* – It is not clear what this means. In Plutarch, the tribunes were merely deprived of their official powers and position; in other words, silenced.

305. *blunt* – slow-witted
306. *mettle* – spirit
309. *tardy form* – pretence of slowness or stupidity
310 – 312. "His show of slowness serves to make his true wit more appealing to those who are willing to listen to his words."

320 – 321. *metal … disposed* – your character (metal) may be worked into a form different from its normal state

319 – 333. In this, the first soliloquy of the play, Cassius discloses to the audience his intention of "seducing" Brutus to join his cause. The revelation presented in this speech is as close as we get in the play to establishing a character who resembles a true villain.

In several hands, in at his windows throw,
As if they came from several citizens,
Writings all tending to the great opinion
That Rome holds of his name; wherein obscurely   330
Caesar's ambition shall be glanced at.
And after this, let Caesar seat him sure,
For we will shake him, or worse days endure.

Exit.

330. *obscurely* – indirectly,
subtly
331. *glanced at* – mentioned;
hinted
332. *seat him sure* – brace
himself securely

Act One
Scene 3

It is the evening of March 14. A fierce storm is raging and the night has been full of strange events. Casca and Cicero discuss the unnatural sights they have witnessed. Cassius persuades Casca to join the plot against Caesar. When Cinna, another conspirator, arrives they discuss the importance of having Brutus join their cause.

3. *sway* – realm. According to the Romans, the Earth was fixed and stable. Everything else, including the sun, revolved around it.

earthquake

5. *scolding* – raging
6. *rived* – split
8. *To be exalted* – as if wanting to be at the same height as
10. *dropping fire* – lightning
20. *Against the Capitol* – opposite the Temple of Jupiter and close to the site of the Senate
21. *glazed* – stared
22. *annoying* – harming
23. *Upon ... women* – into a crowd, a hundred women pale with fear

Rome. A street.

Thunder and lightning. Enter [from different directions] Casca [with his sword drawn] and Cicero.

CICERO: Good even, Casca. Brought you Caesar home?
　　　Why are you breathless, and why stare you so?
CASCA: Are not you moved, when all the sway of earth
　　　Shakes, like a thing unfirm? O Cicero,
　　　I have seen tempests, when the scolding winds
　　　Have rived the knotty oaks, and I have seen
　　　The ambitious ocean swell, and rage, and foam,
　　　To be exalted with the threatening clouds.
　　　But never till tonight, never till now,
　　　Did I go through a tempest dropping fire.　　　　10
　　　Either there is a civil strife in heaven,
　　　Or else the world, too saucy with the gods,
　　　Incenses them to send destruction.
CICERO: Why, saw you anything more wonderful?
CASCA: A common slave, you know him well by sight,
　　　Held up his left hand, which did flame and burn
　　　Like twenty torches joined, and yet his hand,
　　　Not sensible of fire, remained unscorched.
　　　Besides, I have not since put up my sword,
　　　Against the Capitol I met a lion,　　　　　　20
　　　Who glazed upon me, and went surly by,
　　　Without annoying me. And there were drawn
　　　Upon a heap, a hundred ghastly women,
　　　Transformed with their fear, who swore they saw
　　　Men, all in fire, walk up and down the streets.

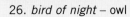

And yesterday, the bird of night did sit,
Even at noon-day, upon the market-place,
Hooting and shrieking. When these prodigies
Do so conjointly meet, let not men say,
"These are their reasons; they are natural,"   30
For, I believe, they are portentous things
Unto the climate that they point upon.

CICERO: Indeed, it is a strange disposed time,
But men may construe things after their fashion,
Clean from the purpose of the things themselves.
Comes Caesar to the Capitol tomorrow?

CASCA: He doth, for he did bid Antonio
Send word to you he would be there tomorrow.

CICERO: Good-night then, Casca.
This disturbed sky is not to walk in.   40

CASCA: Farewell, Cicero.

Exit Cicero. Enter Cassius.

CASSIUS: Who's there?

CASCA: A Roman.

CASSIUS: Casca, by your voice.

CASCA: Your ear is good.
Cassius, what night is this!

CASSIUS: A very pleasing night to honest men.

CASCA: Who ever knew the heavens menace so?

CASSIUS: Those that have known the earth so full of faults.
For my part, I have walked about the streets,   50
Submitting me unto the perilous night,
And, thus unbraced, Casca, as you see,
Have bared my bosom to the thunder-stone.
And when the cross blue lightning seemed to open
The breast of heaven, I did present myself
Even in the aim and very flash of it.

CASCA: But wherefore did you so much tempt the heavens?
It is the part of men to fear and tremble,
When the most mighty gods, by tokens send
Such dreadful heralds to astonish us.   60

CASSIUS: You are dull, Casca,
And those sparks of life that should be in a Roman,
You do want, or else you use not.
You look pale and gaze, and put on fear,
And cast yourself in wonder,
To see the strange impatience of the heavens.

---

26. *bird of night* – owl

29. *conjointly meet* – occur at the same time

31. *portentous* – ominous, foreboding

32. *climate* – region, area

"For Elizabethans, this warning of how language may misrepresent fact, how words — whether involuntarily or on purpose — can falsify phenomenal experience, must have seemed especially striking on the lips of Cicero: acknowledged grand master of the art of persuasion, the greatest orator and rhetorician of the ancient world."
– Anne Barton, British professor, University of Oxford

45. *Your ear is good* – Casca's assessment of Cassius echoes Caesar's admission in the previous scene that "this ear is deaf."

52. *unbraced* – unbuttoned

53. *thunder-stone* – thunderbolt. It was generally believed that, during a storm, a fiery stone was released from the clouds which appeared in the form of lightning.

60. *heralds* – signs; messages

61. *dull* – lacking spirit or intelligence

63. *want* – lack

27

69. *from quality and kind* – contrary to their usual nature
70. *calculate* – prophesy; predict
71. *ordinance* – normal practice as ordained by their nature
72. *preformed* – original; inherent
74. *spirits* – unnatural tendencies
76. *monstrous state* – unnatural state of affairs

"Augury plays an important part in the tragedy, for characters are prone to interpret omens according to their hopes and fears; they unwittingly see reflected in the portents the images of their own passions, and thus both senses and reason are abused."
– D.J. Palmer, professor, University of Hull, Quebec

87. *thews* – sinews; muscles
90. *yoke and sufferance* – willingness to suffer being subjugated to Caesar
94. *save* – except

95 – 106. Cassius asserts that he can free himself from tyranny by killing himself. Because of his Epicurean philosophy, death holds no terror for him. Death, according to his philosophy, is annihilation and freedom from this world's cares.

97. *Therein* – by means of (this dagger)

But if you would consider the true cause,
Why all these fires, why all these gliding ghosts,
Why birds and beasts from quality and kind,
Why old men, fools, and children calculate,   70
Why all these things change from their ordinance,
Their natures and preformed faculties
To monstrous quality, why, you shall find
That heaven hath infused them with these spirits,
To make them instruments of fear and warning,
Unto some monstrous state.
Now could I, Casca, name to thee a man
Most like this dreadful night,
That thunders, lightens, opens graves, and roars,
As doth the lion in the Capitol,   80
A man no mightier than thyself or me,
In personal action, yet prodigious grown,
And fearful, as these strange eruptions are.

CASCA: 'Tis Caesar that you mean.
Is it not, Cassius?

CASSIUS: Let it be who it is, for Romans now
Have thews and limbs like to their ancestors.
But woe the while! Our fathers' minds are dead,
And we are governed with our mothers' spirits.
Our yoke and sufferance show us womanish.   90

CASCA: Indeed, they say the senators tomorrow
Mean to establish Caesar as a king,
And he shall wear his crown by sea and land,
In every place, save here in Italy.

CASSIUS: I know where I will wear this dagger then.
Cassius from bondage will deliver Cassius.
Therein, ye gods, you make the weak most strong;
Therein, ye gods, you tyrants do defeat.
Nor stony tower, nor walls of beaten brass,
Nor airless dungeon, nor strong links of iron,   100
Can be retentive to the strength of spirit.
But life, being weary of these worldly bars,
Never lacks power to dismiss itself.
If I know this, know all the world besides,
That part of tyranny that I do bear,
I can shake off at pleasure.

Thunder still.

CASCA: So can I.
    So every bondman in his own hand bears
    The power to cancel his captivity.
CASSIUS: And why should Caesar be a tyrant then?   110
    Poor man! I know he would not be a wolf,
    But that he sees the Romans are but sheep.
    He were no lion, were not Romans hinds.
    Those that with haste will make a mighty fire,
    Begin it with weak straws. What trash is Rome,
    What rubbish and what offal, when it serves
    For the base matter to illuminate
    So vile a thing as Caesar! But, O grief,
    Where hast thou led me? I, perhaps, speak this
    Before a willing bondman. Then I know   120
    My answer must be made. But I am armed,
    And dangers are to me indifferent.
CASCA: You speak to Casca, and to such a man
    That is no fleering tell-tale. Hold, my hand.
    Be factious for redress of all these griefs,
    And I will set this foot of mine as far
    As who goes farthest.
CASSIUS: There's a bargain made.
    Now know you, Casca, I have moved already
    Some certain of the noblest-minded Romans   130
    To undergo, with me, an enterprise
    Of honourable dangerous consequence;
    And I do know by this, they stay for me
    In Pompey's porch. For now this fearful night,
    There is no stir or walking in the streets;
    And the complexion of the element
    In favour's like the work we have in hand,
    Most bloody, fiery, and most terrible.

Enter Cinna.

CASCA: Stand close awhile, for here comes one in haste.
CASSIUS: 'Tis Cinna. I do know him by his gait.   140
    He is a friend. Cinna, where haste you so?
CINNA: To find out you. Who's that? Metellus Cimber?
CASSIUS: No, it is Casca, one incorporate
    To our attempts. Am I not stayed for, Cinna?
CINNA: I am glad on it.
    What a fearful night is this!
    There's two or three of us have seen strange sights.

108. *bondman* – a person bound to serve another; a slave

113. *hinds* – female deer, peasants, and servants; a wordplay
116. *offal* – garbage

121. *answer* – response to charges of treason. This is assuming that Casca is a willing bondman and will turn Cassius in.
122. *indifferent* – of no concern
124. *fleering* – grinning
125. *Be factious ... griefs* – form a faction or group designed to address these grievances
133. *stay* – wait
136 – 137. "The appearance of the sky is like the plan we are plotting."

140. Despite the foul weather conditions, Cassius can make out the identity of Cinna "by his gait." Cassius' eyesight is formidable indeed. Note what he says later about his vision in Act Five, Scene 3.

143. *incorporate* – united with us

153. *praetor* – magistrate. Brutus held the office of chief praetor, a position just below that of consul. Caesar and Mark Antony were consuls at that time.

praetor's chair

155. *Set* – seal

156. *old Brutus* – See note for Act One, Scene 2, line 169.

160. *hie* – hurry

Pompey's theatre

168 – 170. Casca believes that Brutus' involvement in the plot will work like magic in transforming something base (murdering Caesar) into something precious (a noble cause). Ironically, however, Casca uses the analogy of alchemy, a process whereby a base metal is transformed into gold (which has never been accomplished).

172. *conceited* – expressed

CASSIUS: Am I not stayed for? Tell me.

CINNA: Yes, you are. O Cassius,
    If you could but win the noble Brutus   150
    To our party —

CASSIUS: Be you content. Good Cinna, take this paper,
    And look you lay it in the praetor's chair,
    Where Brutus may but find it, and throw this
    In at his window. Set this up with wax
    Upon old Brutus' statue. All this done,
    Repair to Pompey's porch, where you shall find us.
    Is Decius Brutus and Trebonius there?

CINNA: All but Metellus Cimber, and he's gone
    To seek you at your house. Well, I will hie,   160
    And so bestow these papers as you bade me.

CASSIUS: That done, repair to Pompey's theatre.

Exit Cinna.

    Come, Casca, you and I will yet, ere day
    See Brutus at his house. Three parts of him
    Is ours already, and the man entire
    Upon the next encounter, yields him ours.

CASCA: O, he sits high in all the people's hearts,
    And that which would appear offence in us,
    His countenance, like richest alchemy,
    Will change to virtue and to worthiness.   170

CASSIUS: Him, and his worth, and our great need of him,
    You have right well conceited. Let us go,
    For it is after midnight, and ere day
    We will awake him, and be sure of him.

Exeunt.

₧ ₧ ₧

Act One Considerations

ACT ONE Scene 1

▶ To be effective, a play's opening scene must achieve certain objectives, one of which is to engage the audience's or reader's attention. To what extent is Shakespeare successful in doing so in this play? How does he accomplish this? What other functions are served by this first scene? Explain.

▶ Flavius and Marullus' opinion of Caesar contrasts sharply with that of the mechanicals. In groups of two or more, develop by consensus four statements that describe the two tribunes' attitude toward Caesar.

▶ As elected tribunes, Flavius and Marullus are responsible for protecting the rights of the common people. Imagine you are one of the tribunes, and that you are required to file a report of the day's events. Write a report of the encounter with the mechanicals in which you outline what transpired and the reasons for your actions.

▶ The events of the story of Julius Caesar take place in Rome in 44 B.C.E. However, as this scene illustrates, the play could just as easily be set in Elizabethan England. What evidence is there to support this view? Why, in your opinion, would Shakespeare place this story in two different time periods?

ACT ONE Scene 2

▶ The Romans in Caesar's day were proud that their Republic, established in 510 B.C.E., had lasted for almost five hundred years. This system of government contained checks and balances that prevented power from falling into the hands of just one person. Caesar posed a threat to this proud democratic tradition, but at the same time he provided the Romans with enlightened social reform, stability, and prosperity. Write a newspaper editorial in which you either defend or condemn Caesar's rise to power.

▶ Research Caesar's accomplishments and contributions to Western civilization in general, and to the Roman state in particular. Present your findings to the class.

▶ Two views of Caesar are presented in this scene. Cassius presents one view, and Caesar himself presents the other through his words and actions. Using words and pictures, create two collages illustrating these two opposing views.

▶ Why does Cicero comment upon the proceedings in the marketplace in Greek rather than in Latin? Why has the line "it was Greek to me" become such a well-known expression? What does it indicate about Casca as commentator?

▶ Casca believes that the unnatural occurrences of the night are signs that something bad will happen. Casca's view is a common one. When it is used in literature, this view is called *pathetic fallacy*, which can be defined as the false belief that nature often reflects what is going on in the lives of people. For example: young people fall in love during sunny days in spring; evil deeds are plotted during violent storms; and detectives do much of their work during foggy nights. How valid do you think this belief is? Can you share an experience during which the weather seemed to reflect human events or emotions? Can you think of any recent movies that utilize this device?

▶ If you came across Cassius during the storm and observed his actions, what would you say to him?

▶ In groups of two or more, compile a list of words that you agree describe Cassius. For each word, provide at least one piece of evidence from this scene to support your opinion.

▶ Why do Cassius, Cinna, and Casca want Brutus to join their cause? What does this reveal about what they think of their cause?

Act Two
Scene 1

Rome. Brutus' orchard.

Enter Brutus.

BRUTUS: What, Lucius, ho!
I cannot, by the progress of the stars,
Give guess how near to day — Lucius, I say!
I would it were my fault to sleep so soundly.
When, Lucius, when? Awake, I say! What, Lucius!

Enter Lucius.

LUCIUS: Called you, my lord?
BRUTUS: Get me a taper in my study, Lucius.
When it is lighted, come and call me here.
LUCIUS: I will, my lord.

[Exit.]

BRUTUS: It must be by his death, and for my part,   10
I know no personal cause to spurn at him,
But for the general. He would be crowned.
How that might change his nature, there's the question.
It is the bright day that brings forth the adder,
And that craves wary walking. Crown him? — that —
And then, I grant, we put a sting in him,
That at his will he may do danger with.
The abuse of greatness is, when it disjoins
Remorse from power. And, to speak truth of Caesar,
I have not known when his affections swayed   20
More than his reason. But 'tis a common proof,

It is very early in the morning of the 15th — the ides of March. Brutus is resolved to kill Caesar to prevent him from becoming a tyrant. The conspirators arrive, and together they plot the assassination of Caesar and agree on a number of other related concerns. This scene marks the beginning of Brutus' leadership in the conspiracy. When Brutus is alone, his wife Portia implores him to confide in her the cause of his strange moods. Just as he promises to do so, they are interrupted by Ligarius. Despite his illness, Ligarius is determined to join in the conspiracy.

4. *fault* – weakness to be able

William Shatner, Captain Kirk in the original *Star Trek* series, played Lucius in a 1955 stage production of *Julius Caesar* in Stratford, Ontario.

7. The name *Lucius* comes from the Latin word for *light*. It is appropriate that in his first appearance in the play, Lucius is sent by Brutus to provide light.

12. *general* – general or public good
14. *adder* – poisonous snake (which feeds during the day)
15. *craves* – necessitates
18. *disjoins* – separates

28. *lest ... prevent* –
"because it is likely he will do this (turn his back on his supporters and friends), we need to stop him now before he becomes too powerful"
28. *quarrel* – action (assassination)
29. *colour ... is* – excuse, justification for the way he is now
30. *Fashion* – think of it
30. *augmented* – grown more powerful

"In *Julius Caesar*, the art of persuasion has come to permeate life so completely that people find themselves using it not only to influence others but to deceive themselves. This is true, above all, of Brutus.... In the Orchard soliloquy, Brutus extracts purpose and resolve not from the facts of the situation but from a collection of verbal nothings: from words like 'may' and 'could.'"
– Anne Barton, British professor, University of Oxford

44. *exhalations* – meteors

47. *redress* – make things right
49. *instigations* – letters urging me to action

That lowliness is young ambition's ladder,
Whereto the climber-upward turns his face.
But when he once attains the upmost round,
He then unto the ladder turns his back,
Looks in the clouds, scorning the base degrees
By which he did ascend. So Caesar may.
Then, lest he may, prevent. And, since the quarrel
Will bear no colour for the thing he is,
Fashion it thus: that what he is, augmented,   30
Would run to these, and these extremities.
And therefore think him as a serpent's egg,
Which hatched, would as his kind grow mischievous,
And kill him in the shell.

Enter Lucius.

LUCIUS: The taper burneth in your closet, sir.
Searching the window for a flint, I found
This paper, thus sealed up, and, I am sure,
It did not lie there when I went to bed.

Gives him the letter.

BRUTUS: Get you to bed again. It is not day.
Is not tomorrow, boy, the ides of March?   40
LUCIUS: I know not, sir.
BRUTUS: Look in the calendar, and bring me word.
LUCIUS: I will, sir.

Exit.

BRUTUS: The exhalations whizzing in the air,
Give so much light, that I may read by them.

Opens the letter and reads.

"Brutus thou sleep'st. Awake, and see thyself.
Shall Rome, etc. Speak, strike, redress!"
Brutus, thou sleep'st. Awake!
Such instigations have been often dropped
Where I have took them up.   50
"Shall Rome, etc." Thus must I piece it out.
Shall Rome stand under one man's awe? What Rome?
My ancestors did from the streets of Rome

The Tarquin drive, when he was called a king.
"Speak, strike, redress!" Am I entreated
To speak and strike? O Rome, I make thee promise,
If the redress will follow, thou receivest
Thy full petition at the hand of Brutus.

Enter Lucius.

LUCIUS: Sir, March is wasted fifteen days.

Knocking within.

BRUTUS: 'Tis good. Go to the gate. Somebody knocks.   60

[Exit Lucius.]

Since Cassius first did whet me against Caesar,
I have not slept.
Between the acting of a dreadful thing,
And the first motion, all the interim is
Like a phantasma, or a hideous dream.
The genius and the mortal instruments
Are then in council; and the state of man,
Like to a little kingdom, suffers then
The nature of an insurrection.

Enter Lucius.

LUCIUS: Sir, 'tis your brother Cassius at the door,   70
   Who doth desire to see you.
BRUTUS: Is he alone?
LUCIUS: No, sir, there are more with him.
BRUTUS: Do you know them?
LUCIUS: No, sir, their hats are plucked about their ears,
   And half their faces buried in their cloaks,
   That by no means I may discover them
   By any mark of favour.
BRUTUS: Let 'em enter.

[Exit Lucius.]

They are the faction. O conspiracy,   80
Shamest thou to show thy dangerous brow by night,
When evils are most free? O, then by day
Where wilt thou find a cavern dark enough

58. *full petition* – all that you have petitioned for
61. *whet* – sharpen, set

65. *phantasma* – nightmare vision
66 – 67. *genius ... council* – inner spirit and physical body debate with each other

69. *insurrection* – civil war

70. *brother* – Cassius is married to Brutus' sister, hence they are brothers-in-law.

75. *hats* – It is more likely that large-brimmed hats were worn by Elizabethan actors and not ancient Romans. See note on the Stage Direction in line 199.
77 – 78. *discover ... favour* – determine who they are by looking at their faces

80. *faction* – conspirators

Act Two • Scene 1

85. *affability* – friendliness
86. *path ... on* – go your way, showing yourself as you really are
87. *Erebus* – Hell or Hades is meant. Erebus, however, usually refers to the gloomy region through which the souls of the dead walk on their way to Hades.

"Every play has its problems; but here we cannot even agree upon who the central character is or whether, whoever he is, he is good or bad."
– Mildred E. Hartsock, American professor and scholar

103 – 104. *watchful ... night* – concerns prevent your eyes from closing and allowing you to sleep

109. *fret* – adorn; interlace

112. *great ... on* – considerable distance encroaching upon
113. *Weighing* – considering

118. *swear our resolution* – make a solemn oath
120. *sufferance* – suffering
121. *betimes* – early; in other words, now

To mask thy monstrous visage? Seek none, conspiracy.
Hide it in smiles and affability,
For if thou path, thy native semblance on,
Not Erebus itself were dim enough
To hide thee from prevention.

Enter the conspirators, Cassius, Casca, Decius,
Cinna, Metullus, and Trebonius.

CASSIUS: I think we are too bold upon your rest.
　　Good morrow Brutus. Do we trouble you?　　　　90
BRUTUS: I have been up this hour, awake all night.
　　Know I these men that come along with you?
CASSIUS: Yes, every man of them, and no man here
　　But honours you, and every one doth wish
　　You had but that opinion of yourself
　　Which every noble Roman bears of you.
　　This is Trebonius.
BRUTUS: He is welcome hither.
CASSIUS: This, Decius Brutus.
BRUTUS: He is welcome too.　　　　　　　　　　100
CASSIUS: This, Casca; this, Cinna; and this, Metellus Cimber.
BRUTUS: They are all welcome.
　　What watchful cares do interpose themselves
　　Betwixt your eyes and night?
CASSIUS: Shall I entreat a word?

[Brutus and Cassius whisper.]

DECIUS: Here lies the east. Doth not the day break here?
CASCA: No.
CINNA: O, pardon, sir, it doth, and yon grey lines
　　That fret the clouds are messengers of day.
CASCA: You shall confess that you are both deceived.　　110
　　Here, as I point my sword, the sun arises,
　　Which is a great way growing on the south,
　　Weighing the youthful season of the year.
　　Some two months hence up higher toward the north
　　He first presents his fire; and the high east
　　Stands as the Capitol, directly here.
BRUTUS: Give me your hands all over, one by one.
CASSIUS: And let us swear our resolution.
BRUTUS: No, not an oath. If not the face of men,
　　The sufferance of our souls, the time's abuse, —　　120
　　If these be motives weak, break off betimes,

And every man hence to his idle bed.
So let high-sighted tyranny range on,
Till each man drop by lottery. But if these,
As I am sure they do, bear fire enough
To kindle cowards and to steel with valour
The melting spirits of women, then, countrymen,
What need we any spur but our own cause,
To prick us to redress? What other bond
Than secret Romans, that have spoke the word,   130
And will not palter? And what other oath
Than honesty to honesty engaged,
That this shall be, or we will fall for it?
Swear priests and cowards and men cautelous,
Old feeble carrions, and such suffering souls
That welcome wrongs. Unto bad causes swear
Such creatures as men doubt, but do not stain
The even virtue of our enterprise,
Nor the insuppressive mettle of our spirits,
To think that or our cause or our performance   140
Did need an oath. When every drop of blood
That every Roman bears, and nobly bears,
Is guilty of a several bastardy,
If he do break the smallest particle
Of any promise that hath passed from him.

CASSIUS: But what of Cicero? Shall we sound him?
I think he will stand very strong with us.

CASCA: Let us not leave him out.

CINNA: No, by no means.

METELLUS: O, let us have him, for his silver hairs   150
Will purchase us a good opinion
And buy men's voices to commend our deeds.
It shall be said, his judgment ruled our hands.
Our youths and wildness, shall no whit appear,
But all be buried in his gravity.

BRUTUS: O, name him not. Let us not break with him,
For he will never follow anything
That other men begin.

CASSIUS: Then leave him out.

CASCA: Indeed he is not fit.   160

DECIUS: Shall no man else be touched but only Caesar?

CASSIUS: Decius, well urged. I think it is not meet,
Mark Antony, so well beloved of Caesar,
Should outlive Caesar. We shall find of him
A shrewd contriver. And, you know, his means,
If he improve them, may well stretch so far

123. *high-sighted* – ambitious; proud
124. *lottery* – chance; whim (of the tyrant)
127. *melting* – passive; yielding
129. *To … redress* – to spur us to find a remedy
130. *secret Romans* – Romans able to keep a secret
131. *palter* – waiver; go back on our word
132. *engaged* – promised
134. *cautelous* – deceitful; cautious
135. *carrions* – old persons who look as pale as corpses
138. *even* – steadfast
139. *insuppressive mettle* – unrestrained courage or spirit
140. *or … or* – either … or
141 – 145. "Those who break such an oath would show they are not true Romans."

146. *sound* – test if he is of like mind

On the swearing of an oath amongst the conspirators: "Even in Shakespeare's own work we will search a long time before we find another speech of such purity: so free of all verbal and metaphoric trickery, so simple, and yet so nobly eloquent."
– Sigurd Burckhardt (1916 – 1966), professor, University of California, San Diego

155. *gravity* – dignity; seriousness
156. *break* – confide
165. *contriver* – opponent
165. *means* – powers; resources

As to annoy us all, which to prevent,
Let Antony and Caesar fall together.

BRUTUS: Our course will seem too bloody, Caius Cassius,
To cut the head off, and then hack the limbs,   170
Like wrath in death and envy afterwards,
For Antony is but a limb of Caesar.
Let us be sacrificers, but not butchers, Caius.
We all stand up against the spirit of Caesar,
And in the spirit of men there is no blood.
O, that we then could come by Caesar's spirit,
And not dismember Caesar! But, alas,
Caesar must bleed for it! And, gentle friends,
Let's kill him boldly, but not wrathfully;
Let's carve him as a dish fit for the gods,   180
Not hew him as a carcass fit for hounds.
And let our hearts, as subtle masters do,
Stir up their servants to an act of rage,
And after seem to chide 'em. This shall make
Our purpose necessary and not envious;
Which so appearing to the common eyes,
We shall be called purgers, not murderers.
And for Mark Antony, think not of him,
For he can do no more than Caesar's arm
When Caesar's head is off.   190

CASSIUS: Yet I fear him,
For in the ingrafted love he bears to Caesar —

BRUTUS: Alas, good Cassius, do not think of him.
If he love Caesar, all that he can do
Is to himself, take thought and die for Caesar.
And that were much he should, for he is given
To sports, to wildness, and much company.

TREBONIUS: There is no fear in him. Let him not die,
For he will live, and laugh at this hereafter.

Clock strikes.

BRUTUS: Peace! Count the clock.   200
CASSIUS: The clock hath stricken three.
TREBONIUS: 'Tis time to part.
CASSIUS: But it is doubtful yet,
Whether Caesar will come forth today, or no,
For he is superstitious grown of late,
Quite from the main opinion he held once
Of fantasy, of dreams, and ceremonies.
It may be, these apparent prodigies,

---

171. *Like ... afterwards* – It will appear that we murder first out of anger and then out of malice

RELATED READING

The Fall of Rome – poem by Susan L. Gilbert (page 121)

183. *servants* – i.e., hands

185. *envious* – malicious
187. *purgers* – purifiers; healers
192. *ingrafted* – deep-seated; ingrained

Stage Direction: This is an *anachronism* — a detail that is outside of its proper time period. (Striking clocks were not invented until about the thirteenth century.) Shakespeare often inserted details that helped his audience appreciate what was going on in the dialogue and plot, perhaps for the same reason that many directors stage Shakespeare's plays in modern dress. By combining two time periods on the stage, Shakespeare emphasized the relevance and the timelessness of the play's action.

207. *ceremonies* – portents; omens

The unaccustomed terror of this night,
And the persuasion of his augurers,   210
May hold him from the Capitol today.
DECIUS: Never fear that. If he be so resolved,
I can oversway him, for he loves to hear
That unicorns may be betrayed with trees,
And bears with glasses, elephants with holes,
Lions with toils and men with flatterers.
But, when I tell him he hates flatterers,
He says he does, being then most flattered.
Let me work,
For I can give his humour the true bent,   220
And I will bring him to the Capitol.
CASSIUS: Nay, we will all of us, be there to fetch him.
BRUTUS: By the eighth hour. Is that the uttermost?
CINNA: Be that the uttermost, and fail not then.
METELLUS: Caius Ligarius doth bear Caesar hard,
Who rated him for speaking well of Pompey.
I wonder none of you have thought of him.
BRUTUS: Now, good Metellus, go along by him.
He loves me well, and I have given him reasons.
Send him but hither, and I'll fashion him.   230
CASSIUS: The morning comes upon us.
We'll leave you, Brutus,
And, friends, disperse yourselves, but all remember
What you have said, and show yourselves true Romans.
BRUTUS: Good gentlemen, look fresh and merrily.
Let not our looks put on our purposes,
But bear it as our Roman actors do,
With untired spirits and formal constancy,
And so good morrow to you every one.

Exeunt all but Brutus.

Boy! Lucius! Fast asleep? It is no matter.   240
Enjoy the honey-heavy dew of slumber.
Thou hast no figures nor no fantasies,
Which busy care draws in the brains of men.
Therefore thou sleep'st so sound.

Enter Portia.

PORTIA: Brutus, my lord.
BRUTUS: Portia, what mean you? Wherefore rise you now?
It is not for your health thus to commit

209. *unaccustomed* – unusual; unnatural
210. *augurers* – priests who interpret omens

augurer

213. *oversway* – convince
213 – 216. According to Decius, Caesar loves to hear stories of powerful beasts that can be caught by trickery: a unicorn can be caught by standing in front of a tree and moving away when the unicorn charges; bears can be confused by mirrors; elephants can be captured by digging holes and covering them with branches; lions can be fooled by snares; and, finally, men can be subdued with flattery. Caesar would consider himself to be immune to such weaknesses.
220. *humour* – disposition
225. *bear ... hard* – bears ... ill will
226. *rated* – scolded strongly
236. *put on* – give away
237 – 238. *But ... constancy* – but let us play our parts ... with spirited enthusiasm and dignified composure
242. *figures* – either worrisome calculations or creations of the imagination

Portia

258. *wafture* – dismissive waving

261. *withal* – furthermore
262. *humour* – moodiness

273. *physical* – healthy
274. *unbraced* – with doublet undone
274. *humours* – dampness
277 – 278. *contagion ... air* – It was believed that the night air posed more danger of contracting diseases than the daytime air, which was purified by the sun.

Your weak condition to the raw cold morning.

PORTIA: Nor for yours neither. You have ungently, Brutus,
Stole from my bed; and yesternight, at supper,   250
You suddenly arose, and walked about,
Musing and sighing, with your arms across,
And when I asked you what the matter was,
You stared upon me with ungentle looks.
I urged you further. Then you scratched your head,
And too impatiently stamped with your foot.
Yet I insisted, yet you answered not,
But, with an angry wafture of your hand,
Gave sign for me to leave you. So I did,
Fearing to strengthen that impatience   260
Which seemed too much enkindled, and withal
Hoping it was but an effect of humour,
Which sometime hath his hour with every man.
It will not let you eat, nor talk, nor sleep,
And could it work so much upon your shape
As it hath much prevailed on your condition,
I should not know you Brutus. Dear my lord,
Make me acquainted with your cause of grief.

BRUTUS: I am not well in health, and that is all.

PORTIA: Brutus is wise, and were he not in health,   270
He would embrace the means to come by it.

BRUTUS: Why, so I do. Good Portia, go to bed.

PORTIA: Is Brutus sick and is it physical
To walk unbraced and suck up the humours
Of the dank morning? What, is Brutus sick?
And will he steal out of his wholesome bed,
To dare the vile contagion of the night
And tempt the rheumy and unpurged air
To add unto his sickness? No, my Brutus.
You have some sick offence within your mind,   280
Which, by the right and virtue of my place,
I ought to know of. And, upon my knees,
I charm you, by my once commended beauty,
By all your vows of love, and that great vow
Which did incorporate and make us one,
That you unfold to me, your self, your half,
Why you are heavy, and what men tonight
Have had to resort to you; for here have been
Some six or seven, who did hide their faces
Even from darkness.   290

BRUTUS: Kneel not, gentle Portia.

PORTIA: I should not need, if you were gentle Brutus.

Within the bond of marriage, tell me, Brutus,
Is it excepted I should know no secrets
That appertain to you? Am I your self
But, as it were in sort or limitation,
To keep with you at meals, comfort your bed,
And talk to you sometimes? Dwell I but in the suburbs
Of your good pleasure? If it be no more,
Portia is Brutus' harlot, not his wife.   300
BRUTUS: You are my true and honourable wife,
As dear to me as are the ruddy drops
That visit my sad heart.
PORTIA: If this were true, then should I know this secret.
I grant I am a woman, but withal
A woman that Lord Brutus took to wife.
I grant I am a woman, but withal
A woman well reputed, Cato's daughter.
Think you I am no stronger than my sex,
Being so fathered and so husbanded?   310
Tell me your counsels, I will not disclose 'em.
I have made strong proof of my constancy,
Giving myself a voluntary wound
Here, in the thigh. Can I bear that with patience,
And not my husband's secrets?
BRUTUS: O ye gods,
Render me worthy of this noble wife!

Knocking within.

Hark, hark! One knocks. Portia, go in awhile,
And by and by thy bosom shall partake
The secrets of my heart.   320
All my engagements, I will construe to thee,
All the charactery of my sad brows.
Leave me with haste.

Exit Portia. Enter Lucius and Ligarius.

Lucius, who's that knocks?
LUCIUS: Here is a sick man that would speak with you.
BRUTUS: Caius Ligarius, that Metellus spake of.
Boy, stand aside. Caius Ligarius, how?
LIGARIUS: Vouchsafe good morrow from a feeble tongue.
BRUTUS: O, what a time have you chose out, brave Caius
To wear a kerchief! Would you were not sick.   330
LIGARIUS: I am not sick, if Brutus have in hand

---

294. *excepted* – excluded from the marriage agreement that

296. *sort or limitation* – Portia continues with the legal jargon introduced with the words *bond* and *excepted*. She asks if she is somehow contracted and limited in her role as a wife.

298. *suburbs* – another detail more familiar to the Elizabethan audience than faithful to the Roman time period. Shakespeare's audience recognized that houses of ill-repute were located in the suburbs of London.

300. *harlot* – prostitute
302. *ruddy drops* – blood
308. *Cato* – Marcus Cato, Brutus' uncle and father-in-law, was an ally of Pompey and one of the last holdouts in the civil war against Caesar. Rather than face capture, Cato committed suicide.

321. *engagements* – commitments
321. *construe* – explain
322. *charactery* – that which is written; the cause

328. *Vouchsafe* – please accept
330. *wear a kerchief* – be sick

Act Two • Scene 1

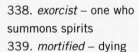

Any exploit worthy the name of honour.

BRUTUS: Such an exploit have I in hand, Ligarius,
Had you a healthful ear to hear of it.

LIGARIUS: By all the gods that Romans bow before,
I here discard my sickness! Soul of Rome!
Brave son, derived from honourable loins!
Thou like an exorcist, hast conjured up
My mortified spirit. Now bid me run,
And I will strive with things impossible,   340
Yea get the better of them. What's to do?

BRUTUS: A piece of work
That will make sick men whole.

LIGARIUS: But are not some whole that we must make sick?

BRUTUS: That must we also. What it is, my Caius,
I shall unfold to thee, as we are going
To whom it must be done.

LIGARIUS: Set on your foot,
And with a heart new-fired I follow you,
To do I know not what, but it sufficeth   350
That Brutus leads me on.

Thunder.

BRUTUS: Follow me, then.

Exeunt.

Act Two
Scene 2

Caesar's house.

Thunder and lightning.
Enter Julius Caesar in his nightgown.

CAESAR: Nor heaven nor earth,
Have been at peace tonight.
Thrice hath Calpurnia in her sleep cried out,
"Help, ho! They murder Caesar!" Who's within?

Enter a Servant.

SERVANT: My lord?
CAESAR: Go bid the priests do present sacrifice
And bring me their opinions of success.
SERVANT: I will, my lord.

Exit [Servant]. Enter Calpurnia.

CALPURNIA: What mean you, Caesar? Think you to walk forth?
You shall not stir out of your house today.   10
CAESAR: Caesar shall forth. The things that threatened me
Never looked but on my back. When they shall see
The face of Caesar, they are vanished.
CALPURNIA: Caesar, I never stood on ceremonies,
Yet now they fright me. There is one within,
Besides the things that we have heard and seen,
Recounts most horrid sights seen by the watch.
A lioness hath whelped in the streets,
And graves have yawned, and yielded up their dead.
Fierce fiery warriors fight upon the clouds,   20
In ranks and squadrons and right form of war
Which drizzled blood upon the Capitol.

It is early morning, the ides of March. Calpurnia has dreamt that Caesar has been murdered. Caesar's augurers advise him not to venture forth, but despite the signs and his wife's appeals Caesar is determined to go to the Senate. He finally relents, however, and agrees to stay home. Decius arrives and reinterprets Calpurnia's dream. Decius convinces Caesar to go to the Senate. They are joined by the other conspirators and together, like friends, they leave for the Capitol.

6. *present* – immediate

11 – 13. Caesar can be considered a true tragic hero in that he suffers from what the Greeks called *hubris* – excess of pride or will. Hubris is the sense of confidence that people have when they feel they cannot be stopped, defeated, or affected by anything around them. This excessive confidence, when combined with a bad choice, sometimes leads to tragedy.

14. *stood on ceremonies* – attached importance to omens
18. *whelped* – given birth
19. *yawned* – opened up
21. *right … war* – as if they were actually engaged in a war

30. Caesar, as is befitting a head of state, either speaks of himself in the first-person plural (us, our, we) or in the third person (Caesar). This convention should not be interpreted as a sign of arrogance.

31. *Are to* – apply to

32 – 33. Calpurnia expresses a view commonly held by the Elizabethans that nature reflects and parallels what is occurring in the lives of people. The unnatural events of the evening described in lines 15 to 26 can be explained by the fact that, during the night, conspirators were plotting to kill Caesar. According to the Elizabethans, plotting to kill a ruler or king is a most unnatural act.

RELATED READING

Calpurnia and Portia – literary essay by Sarojini Shintri (page 122)

The noise of battle hurtled in the air,
Horses did neigh, and dying men did groan,
And ghosts did shriek and squeal about the streets.
O Caesar! These things are beyond all use,
And I do fear them.
CAESAR: What can be avoided
Whose end is purposed by the mighty gods?
Yet Caesar shall go forth, for these predictions   30
Are to the world in general as to Caesar.
CALPURNIA: When beggars die, there are no comets seen.
The heavens themselves blaze forth the death of princes.
CAESAR: Cowards die many times before their deaths;
The valiant never taste of death but once.
Of all the wonders that I yet have heard,
It seems to me most strange that men should fear,
Seeing that death, a necessary end,
Will come when it will come.

Enter a Servant.

What say the augurers?   40
SERVANT: They would not have you to stir forth today.
Plucking the entrails of an offering forth,
They could not find a heart within the beast.

46

CAESAR: The gods do this in shame of cowardice.
      Caesar should be a beast without a heart,
      If he should stay at home today for fear.
      No Caesar shall not. Danger knows full well
      That Caesar is more dangerous than he.
      We are two lions littered in one day,
      And I the elder and more terrible,   50
      And Caesar shall go forth.
CALPURNIA: Alas, my lord,
      Your wisdom is consumed in confidence.
      Do not go forth today. Call it my fear
      That keeps you in the house and not your own.
      We'll send Mark Antony to the Senate House
      And he shall say, you are not well today.
      Let me upon my knee, prevail in this.
CAESAR: Mark Antony shall say I am not well,
      And for thy humour, I will stay at home.   60

Enter Decius.

      Here's Decius Brutus, he shall tell them so.
DECIUS: Caesar, all hail! Good morrow, worthy Caesar.
      I come to fetch you to the Senate House.

53. Calpurnia comments on Caesar's hubris. See note on page 45 for lines 11 – 13.

75. *Lest* – for fear that

80. *stays* – keeps

83. *lusty* – hardy and happy

85. *portents* – signs

89. Decius flatters Caesar into accepting his interpretation of the vision. In doing so, he diverts Caesar from realizing that his interpretation is not significantly different from Calpurnia's. Caesar's failing is that he does not inquire as to whom the vision would be "fair and fortunate."

94. Decius refers to the practice of people dipping their handkerchiefs in the blood of martyrs and keeping the bloody napkins as remembrances of the martyrs.

CAESAR: And you are come in very happy time,
　　　　To bear my greeting to the senators
　　　　And tell them that I will not come today.
　　　　Cannot, is false, and that I dare not, falser.
　　　　I will not come today. Tell them so Decius.
CALPURNIA: Say he is sick.
CAESAR: Shall Caesar send a lie?　　　　　　　　　　70
　　　　Have I in conquest stretched mine arm so far
　　　　To be afraid to tell greybeards the truth?
　　　　Decius, go tell them, Caesar will not come.
DECIUS: Most mighty Caesar, let me know some cause,
　　　　Lest I be laughed at when I tell them so.
CAESAR: The cause is in my will. I will not come.
　　　　That is enough to satisfy the Senate.
　　　　But for your private satisfaction,
　　　　Because I love you, I will let you know.
　　　　Calpurnia here my wife, stays me at home.　　80
　　　　She dreamt tonight she saw my statue,
　　　　Which like a fountain with an hundred spouts
　　　　Did run pure blood, and many lusty Romans
　　　　Came smiling, and did bathe their hands in it.
　　　　And these does she apply, for warnings, and portents,
　　　　And evils imminent. And on her knee
　　　　Hath begged, that I will stay at home today.
DECIUS: This dream is all amiss interpreted.
　　　　It was a vision, fair and fortunate.
　　　　Your statue spouting blood in many pipes,　　90
　　　　In which so many smiling Romans bathed,
　　　　Signifies, that from you great Rome shall suck
　　　　Reviving blood, and that great men shall press
　　　　For tinctures, stains, relics and cognizance.
　　　　This by Calpurnia's dream is signified.
CAESAR: And this way have you well expounded it.
DECIUS: I have, when you have heard what I can say,
　　　　And know it now. The Senate have concluded
　　　　To give this day a crown to mighty Caesar.
　　　　If you shall send them word you will not come,　　100
　　　　Their minds may change. Besides, it were a mock
　　　　Apt to be rendered, for someone to say,
　　　　"Break up the Senate till another time,
　　　　When Caesar's wife shall meet with better dreams."
　　　　If Caesar hide himself, shall they not whisper
　　　　"Lo, Caesar is afraid"?
　　　　Pardon me, Caesar, for my dear dear love

48

To your proceeding, bids me tell you this,
And reason to my love is liable.
CAESAR: How foolish do your fears seem now Calpurnia!   110
I am ashamed I did yield to them.
Give me my robe, for I will go.

Enter Brutus, Ligarius, Metullus, Casca,
Trebonius, Cinna, and Publius.

And look where Publius is come to fetch me.
PUBLIUS: Good morrow, Caesar.
CAESAR: Welcome, Publius.
What, Brutus, are you stirred so early too?
Good morrow, Casca. Caius Ligarius,
Caesar was never so much your enemy,
As that same ague which hath made you lean.
What is it o'clock?   120
BRUTUS: Caesar, 'tis strucken eight.
CAESAR: I thank you for your pains and courtesy.

Enter Antony.

See, Antony that revels long a-nights,
Is notwithstanding up. Good morrow, Antony.
ANTONY: So to most noble Caesar.
CAESAR: Bid them prepare within.
I am to blame to be thus waited for.
Now Cinna, now Metellus. What, Trebonius.
I have an hour's talk in store for you.
Remember that you call on me today.   130
Be near me that I may remember you.
TREBONIUS: Caesar, I will. *[Aside.]* And so near will I be,
That your best friends shall wish I had been further.
CAESAR: Good friends go in, and taste some wine with me,
And we, like friends, will straightway go together.
BRUTUS: *[Aside.]* That every like is not the same, O Caesar.
The heart of Brutus earns to think upon.

Exeunt.

108. *proceeding* – advancement
109. "My love for you is stronger than my better judgment."

"Caesar appears at his most amiable in the little scene with the conspirators before they leave for the Capitol, and he does so because he is there sympathetic toward the others in his feeling for their personal lives. This small scene throws into sharp contrast the violence of the murder which immediately follows and confirms ... that the prime concern of the play is not the breach of civil peace but with the breaking of the bonds of humanity in the killing of Caesar."
– Joan Rees (b. 1923), British scholar, professor, University of Birmingham

119. *ague* – illness
124. *notwithstanding* – nevertheless

The final moment of this scene depends on *dramatic irony* for its effectiveness. Dramatic irony occurs when the reader or the audience knows something of which one or more persons on the stage is not aware. We know the true nature and intentions of the conspirators. That Caesar should consider them friends is ironic.

136. *like ... same* – Brutus refers to one of Shakespeare's most popular themes — the discrepancy between appearance and reality. He grieves (earns) that he has to put on a show of friendship rather than exhibit the real thing.

Act Two • Scene 2

Artemidorus, a friend to Caesar, stands ready with a letter that, if read by Caesar, will expose the conspiracy and save his life.

Act Two
Scene 3

A street near the Capitol.

Enter Artemidorus [reading a paper].

ARTEMIDORUS: "Caesar, beware of Brutus; take heed of Cassius; come not near Casca; have an eye to Cinna; trust not Trebonius; mark well Metellus Cimber. Decius Brutus loves thee not. Thou hast wronged Caius Ligarius. There is but one mind in all these men, and it is bent against Caesar. If thou beest not immortal, look about you. Security gives way to conspiracy. The mighty gods defend thee!

Thy lover, Artemidorus."

Here will I stand, till Caesar pass along,   10
And as a suitor will I give him this.
My heart laments that virtue cannot live
Out of the teeth of emulation.
If thou read this, O Caesar, thou mayst live.
If not, the Fates with traitors do contrive.

Exit.

7. *Security ... conspiracy* – overconfidence provides conspirators with opportunity to do their will

11. *suitor* – one with a petition to present

13. *Out ... emulation* – beyond the ravenous jaws (reach) of envious persons

15. *contrive* – join sides

Act Two
Scene 4

A street before the house of Brutus.

It is obvious that Brutus has told Portia of the conspirators' plan to kill Caesar. Anxious about her husband's safety, she sends Lucius for news from the Capitol. She speaks briefly to the Soothsayer, who mentions that he will try to warn Caesar to be especially careful on this day.

Enter Portia and Lucius.

PORTIA: I prithee, boy, run to the Senate House.
　　　Stay not to answer me, but get thee gone.
　　　Why dost thou stay?
LUCIUS: To know my errand, madam.
PORTIA: I would have had thee there and here again,
　　　Ere I can tell thee what thou shouldst do there.
　　　O constancy, be strong upon my side.
　　　Set a huge mountain 'tween my heart and tongue!
　　　I have a man's mind, but a woman's might.
　　　How hard it is for women to keep counsel!　　　10
　　　Art thou here yet?
LUCIUS: Madam, what should I do?
　　　Run to the Capitol, and nothing else?
　　　And so return to you, and nothing else?
PORTIA: Yes, bring me word, boy, if thy lord look well,
　　　For he went sickly forth. And take good note
　　　What Caesar doth, what suitors press to him.
　　　Hark, boy, what noise is that?
LUCIUS: I hear none, madam.
PORTIA: Prithee listen well.　　　20
　　　I heard a bustling rumour, like a fray,
　　　And the wind brings it from the Capitol.
LUCIUS: Sooth, madam, I hear nothing.

Enter the Soothsayer.

PORTIA: Come hither, fellow. Which way hast thou been?
SOOTHSAYER: At mine own house, good lady.

7. *constancy* – self-control

21. *bustling ... fray* – loud commotion like a fight
23. *Sooth* – in truth

34. *beseech* – request
34. *befriend himself* – do himself a service
37. *chance* – happen

40. *praetors* – judges

42. *void* – empty

PORTIA: What is it o'clock?
SOOTHSAYER: About the ninth hour, lady.
PORTIA: Is Caesar yet gone to the Capitol?
SOOTHSAYER: Madam, not yet. I go to take my stand,
   To see him pass on to the Capitol.   30
PORTIA: Thou hast some suit to Caesar, hast thou not?
SOOTHSAYER: That I have, lady, if it will please Caesar
   To be so good to Caesar as to hear me,
   I shall beseech him to befriend himself.
PORTIA: Why, know'st thou any harm's intended towards him?
SOOTHSAYER: None that I know will be,
   Much that I fear may chance.
   Good morrow to you. Here the street is narrow.
   The throng that follows Caesar at the heels,
   Of senators, of praetors, common suitors,   40
   Will crowd a feeble man almost to death.
   I'll get me to a place more void, and there
   Speak to great Caesar as he comes along.

Exit.

PORTIA: I must go in.
     Ay me, how weak a thing
The heart of woman is! O Brutus,
The heavens speed thee in thine enterprise!
Sure, the boy heard me. Brutus hath a suit
That Caesar will not grant. O, I grow faint.
Run, Lucius, and commend me to my lord.   50
Say I am merry. Come to me again,
And bring me word what he doth say to thee.

               Exeunt.

50. *commend me* – give my love

Act Two Considerations

ACT TWO Scene 1

▶ Brutus readily admits that Caesar has done nothing yet to deserve being killed. Caesar, however, has the potential to become a tyrant, and therefore Brutus feels justified in thinking of Caesar as a "serpent's egg" that should be crushed in its shell. What do you think of the ethics of this argument? Are we justified in taking action before a crime is committed?

▶ In pairs, brainstorm a list of words to describe either Brutus' or Portia's character as it is revealed in this scene. Once you have completed the list, go back to the scene and find evidence to support your conclusions.

▶ What purposes are served in the play by the scene between Brutus and Portia?

▶ What does the exchange between Brutus and Ligarius reveal about Brutus?

ACT TWO Scene 2

▶ Caesar prides himself on being constant and resolute. To what extent do you think this self-assessment is true? Provide evidence to support your opinion.

▶ Based on what you have seen of Caesar so far, in your opinion how superstitious is he? Explain.

▶ Most people today would consider Caesar to be overly proud and arrogant. The audience in Shakespeare's day, however, would consider Caesar to be acting and talking in an appropriate manner, given his rank. Imagine you are part of that audience. Describe in positive terms what is revealed of Caesar in this scene. What effect does this view have on our interpretation of the conspirators' character and intentions?

ACT TWO Scenes 3 and 4

▶ What primary purpose is served by these two short scenes?

▶ What does Scene 4 reveal about Portia's state of mind and character? If you were her friend, what advice would you give to help her cope with the situation?

Act Three
Scene 1

Rome. Before the Capitol.

Alex
Ingo
Ryn

Flourish. Enter Caesar, Brutus, Cassius, Casca, Decius, Metellus,
Trebonius, Cinna, Antony, Lepidus, Artemidorus,
[Popilius], Publius, and the Soothsayer.

CAESAR: *[To the Soothsayer.]* The ides of March are come.
SOOTHSAYER: Ay, Caesar, but not gone.
ARTEMIDORUS: Hail, Caesar! Read this schedule.
DECIUS: Trebonius doth desire you to over-read,
    At your best leisure, this his humble suit.
ARTEMIDORUS: O Caesar, read mine first, for mine's a suit
    That touches Caesar nearer. Read it, great Caesar.
CAESAR: What touches us ourself shall be last served.
ARTEMIDORUS: Delay not, Caesar. Read it instantly.
CAESAR: What, is the fellow mad?   10
PUBLIUS: Sirrah, give place.
CASSIUS: What, urge you your petitions in the street?
    Come to the Capitol.

       [Caesar and the rest following, go forward.]

POPILIUS: I wish your enterprise today may thrive.
CASSIUS: What enterprise, Popilius?
POPILIUS: Fare you well.

       [Leaves Cassius and advances to Caesar.]

BRUTUS: What said Popilius Lena?
CASSIUS: He wished today our enterprise might thrive.
    I fear our purpose is discovered.

Both the Soothsayer and Artemidorus attempt to warn Caesar that his life is in danger. Caesar, however, pays no heed to their warnings. He enters the Capitol with the conspirators, who encircle and kill him with their knives. Antony, having been given assurances that his life is not threatened, arrives and is treated as a friend by the conspirators. Brutus grants him permission to speak at Caesar's funeral. When alone, Antony prophesies that Italy will be wracked with civil war and that Caesar's death will be avenged.

3. *schedule* – document
4. *over-read* – read over

RELATED READING

The Ides of March – poem by C.P. Cavafy (page 120)

11. *Sirrah* – a mildly contemptuous way of saying "good sir"

12. In Plutarch, Shakespeare's source, the press of the crowd physically prevents Caesar from reading Artemidorus' petition.

21. *be sudden* – act quickly
21. *prevention* – being stopped

32. *addressed* – prepared
33. *rears* – raises; strikes

36. *puissant* – powerful

40. *couchings* – kneeling
42 – 43. *preordinance ... children* – that which has been established and preordained since the beginning of time to be something frivolous and not lasting
43. *fond* – foolish
44. *rebel blood* – untrue, inconstant nature

"It cost Shakespeare no pang to write Caesar down for the merely technical purpose of writing Brutus up. And what a Brutus!"
– George Bernard Shaw (1856 – 1950), Irish playwright, satirist, and critic

51. *cause* – reason
55. *repealing* – recalling

BRUTUS: Look how he makes to Caesar. Mark him.   20
CASSIUS: Casca be sudden, for we fear prevention.
    Brutus, what shall be done? If this be known,
    Cassius or Caesar never shall turn back,
    For I will slay myself.
BRUTUS: Cassius, be constant.
    Popilius Lena speaks not of our purposes,
    For look, he smiles, and Caesar doth not change.
CASSIUS: Trebonius knows his time, for look you Brutus,
    He draws Mark Antony out of the way.

[Exeunt Antony and Trebonius.]

DECIUS: Where is Metellus Cimber? Let him go,   30
    And presently prefer his suit to Caesar.
BRUTUS: He is addressed. Press near and second him.
CINNA: Casca, you are the first that rears your hand.
CAESAR: Are we all ready? What is now amiss
    That Caesar and his senate must redress?
METELLUS: Most high, most mighty, and most puissant Caesar,
    Metellus Cimber throws before thy seat
    An humble heart, —

[Metellus kneeling.]

CAESAR: I must prevent thee, Cimber.
    These couchings and these lowly courtesies   40
    Might fire the blood of ordinary men,
    And turn preordinance and first decree
    Into the law of children. Be not fond,
    To think that Caesar bears such rebel blood
    That will be thawed from the true quality
    With that which melteth fools — I mean, sweet words,
    Low-crooked court'sies and base spaniel-fawning.
    Thy brother by decree is banished.
    If thou dost bend, and pray, and fawn for him,
    I spurn thee like a cur out of my way.   50
    Know, Caesar doth not wrong, nor without cause
    Will he be satisfied.
METELLUS: Is there no voice more worthy than my own
    To sound more sweetly in great Caesar's ear
    For the repealing of my banished brother?
BRUTUS: I kiss thy hand, but not in flattery, Caesar,
    Desiring thee that Publius Cimber may
    Have an immediate freedom of repeal.

CAESAR: What, Brutus!
CASSIUS: Pardon, Caesar, Caesar, pardon.   60
    As low as to thy foot doth Cassius fall,
    To beg enfranchisement for Publius Cimber.
CAESAR: I could be well moved, if I were as you.
    If I could pray to move, prayers would move me;
    But I am constant as the Northern Star,
    Of whose true-fixed and resting quality,
    There is no fellow in the firmament.
    The skies are painted with unnumbered sparks,
    They are all fire and every one doth shine,
    But, there's but one in all doth hold his place.   70
    So, in the world; 'tis furnished well with men,
    And men are flesh and blood, and apprehensive.
    Yet in the number I do know but one
    That unassailable holds on his rank,
    Unshaked of motion. And that I am he,
    Let me a little show it, even in this.
    That I was constant Cimber should be banished,
    And constant do remain to keep him so.
CINNA: O Caesar, —
CAESAR: Hence! Wilt thou lift up Olympus?   80
DECIUS: Great Caesar —
CAESAR: Doth not Brutus bootless kneel?
CASCA: Speak, hands for me!

[Casca first, and then the other Conspirators stab Caesar.
Then Brutus stabs Caesar.]

CAESAR: *Et tu, Brute?* Then fall, Caesar.

Dies.

CINNA: Liberty! Freedom! Tyranny is dead!
    Run hence, proclaim, cry it about the streets.
CASSIUS: Some to the common pulpits, and cry out
    "Liberty, freedom, and enfranchisement!"
BRUTUS: People and senators, be not affrighted;
    Fly not, stand still! Ambition's debt is paid.   90
CASCA: Go to the pulpit, Brutus.
DECIUS: And Cassius too.
BRUTUS: Where's Publius?
CINNA: Here, quite confounded with this mutiny.
METELLUS: Stand fast together, lest some friend of Caesar's
    Should chance —

62. *enfranchisement* – restoration of rights as a citizen
64. *pray to move* – plead with others to go back on their decisions

65. *Northern Star* – Before the rise of modern navigational equipment, sailors used the Pole Star to navigate by. It was unique in the heavens ("no fellow in the firmament") because it remained fixed and changeless in position.

72. *apprehensive* – capable of apprehending; reasoning
74. *unassailable* – not open to attack
80. Caesar implies that it would be as impossible to lift Mount Olympus as it would be to get him to change his mind.
82. *bootless* – in vain

84. *Et tu, Brute?* – Latin for "And even you, Brutus?" According to Plutarch, Caesar's last words were in Greek.

87. *pulpits* – platforms from which speakers would address the crowds
90. *Ambition's ... paid* – the penalty for being ambitious. In other words, ambition has received what it deserves and there will be no more killings.
94. *confounded* – in a state of shock or confusion

102. *abide* – wait to be held responsible

"*Julius Caesar* is about the tragic consequences that befall idealism when it attempts to enter the sphere of action. It is perhaps also a comment on the futility and dangerousness of action in general."
– Mary McCarthy (1912 – 1989), American theatre critic

110. *drawing* – prolonging
114. abridged – cut short

124. *in sport* – in a play
125. *basis* – Ironically, Caesar was killed at the base of Pompey's statue. The basis would be the pedestal upon which it stands.
128. *knot* – group

129. It has been noted that American revolutionist Patrick Henry's famous line "Give me liberty or give me death" was inspired by Cassius' speech.

BRUTUS: Talk not of standing. Publius, good cheer.
　　　　There is no harm intended to your person,
　　　　Nor to no Roman else. So tell them, Publius.
CASSIUS: And leave us, Publius, lest that the people,　　　100
　　　　Rushing on us, should do your age some mischief.
BRUTUS: Do so, and let no man abide this deed,
　　　　But we the doers.

Enter Trebonius.

CASSIUS: Where is Antony?
TREBONIUS: Fled to his house amazed.
　　　　Men, wives and children stare, cry out, and run
　　　　As it were doomsday.
BRUTUS: Fates, we will know your pleasures.
　　　　That we shall die we know; 'tis but the time
　　　　And drawing days out, that men stand upon.　　　110
CASSIUS: Why, he that cuts off twenty years of life
　　　　Cuts off so many years of fearing death.
BRUTUS: Grant that, and then is death a benefit.
　　　　So are we Caesar's friends, that have abridged
　　　　His time of fearing death. Stoop Romans, stoop,
　　　　And let us bathe our hands in Caesar's blood
　　　　Up to the elbows, and besmear our swords.
　　　　Then walk we forth, even to the market-place,
　　　　And, waving our red weapons over our heads,
　　　　Let's all cry, "Peace, freedom and liberty!"　　　120
CASSIUS: Stoop then, and wash. How many ages hence
　　　　Shall this our lofty scene be acted over
　　　　In states unborn, and accents yet unknown!
BRUTUS: How many times shall Caesar bleed in sport,
　　　　That now on Pompey's basis lies along
　　　　No worthier than the dust!
CASSIUS: So oft as that shall be,
　　　　So often shall the knot of us be called
　　　　The men that gave their country liberty.
DECIUS: What, shall we forth?　　　130
CASSIUS: Ay, every man away.
　　　　Brutus shall lead, and we will grace his heels
　　　　With the most boldest and best hearts of Rome.

Enter a Servant.

BRUTUS: Soft, who comes here? A friend of Antony's.
SERVANT: Thus, Brutus, did my master bid me kneel.

Thus did Mark Antony bid me fall down.
And being prostrate, thus he bade me say:
Brutus is noble, wise, valiant, and honest.
Caesar was mighty, bold, royal, and loving.
Say, I love Brutus, and I honour him.   140
Say, I feared Caesar, honoured him and loved him.
If Brutus will vouchsafe, that Antony
May safely come to him, and be resolved
How Caesar hath deserved to lie in death,
Mark Antony shall not love Caesar dead
So well as Brutus living, but will follow
The fortunes and affairs of noble Brutus
Thorough the hazards of this untrod state
With all true faith. So says my master Antony.

BRUTUS: Thy master is a wise and valiant Roman.   150
I never thought him worse.
Tell him, so please him come unto this place,
He shall be satisfied, and by my honour,
Depart untouched.

SERVANT: I'll fetch him presently.

Exit Servant.

BRUTUS: I know that we shall have him well to friend.

CASSIUS: I wish we may, but yet have I a mind
That fears him much, and my misgiving still
Falls shrewdly to the purpose.

Enter Antony.

BRUTUS: But here comes Antony.
Welcome, Mark Antony.   160

ANTONY: O mighty Caesar! Dost thou lie so low?
Are all thy conquests, glories, triumphs, spoils,
Shrunk to this little measure? Fare thee well.
I know not, gentlemen, what you intend,
Who else must be let blood, who else is rank.
If I myself, there is no hour so fit
As Caesar's death hour, nor no instrument
Of half that worth, as those your swords, made rich
With the most noble blood of all this world.   170
I do beseech ye, if you bear me hard,
Now, whilst your purpled hands do reek and smoke,
Fulfil your pleasure. Live a thousand years,
I shall not find myself so apt to die.

142. *vouchsafe* – promise

148. *untrod state* – uncertain state of affairs

"Shakespeare keeps [Antony] in ambush throughout the first part of the play. Up to the time when he faces the triumphant conspirators he speaks just thirty-three words. But there have already been no less than seven separate references to him, all significant."
– Harley Granville-Barker (1877 – 1946), British playwright, producer, and critic

158 – 159. Cassius has a bad feeling about Antony and maintains that in the past, whenever he had a bad feeling about something, he was invariably right.
164. *little measure* – small space that your body now takes up
166. *rank* – diseased and in need of curing by blood-letting
171. *hard* – ill will
174. *apt* – ready

61

bayed hart

No place will please me so, no mean of death,
As here by Caesar, and by you cut off,
The choice and master spirits of this age.
BRUTUS: O Antony! Beg not your death of us.
    Though now we must appear bloody and cruel,
    As by our hands, and this our present act   180
    You see we do, yet see you but our hands
    And this the bleeding business they have done.
    Our hearts you see not. They are pitiful,
    And pity to the general wrong of Rome —
    As fire drives out fire, so pity, pity —
    Hath done this deed on Caesar. For your part,
    To you, our swords have leaden points, Mark Antony.
    Our arms, in strength of malice, and our hearts
    Of brothers' temper, do receive you in
    With all kind love, good thoughts, and reverence.   190
CASSIUS: Your voice shall be as strong as any man's
    In the disposing of new dignities.
BRUTUS: Only be patient till we have appeased
    The multitude, beside themselves with fear,
    And then, we will deliver you the cause,
    Why I, that did love Caesar when I struck him,
    Have thus proceeded.
ANTONY: I doubt not of your wisdom.
    Let each man render me his bloody hand.
    First, Marcus Brutus, will I shake with you   200
    Next, Caius Cassius do I take your hand.
    Now, Decius Brutus yours. Now yours Metellus.
    Yours Cinna, and my valiant Casca, yours.
    Though last, not last in love, yours good Trebonius.
    Gentlemen all — alas, what shall I say?
    My credit now stands on such slippery ground,
    That one of two bad ways you must conceit me,
    Either a coward or a flatterer.
    That I did love thee Caesar, O, 'tis true!
    If then thy spirit look upon us now,   210
    Shall it not grieve thee dearer than thy death,
    To see thy Antony making his peace,
    Shaking the bloody fingers of thy foes?
    Most noble, in the presence of thy corse,
    Had I as many eyes as thou hast wounds,
    Weeping as fast as they stream forth thy blood,
    It would become me better, than to close
    In terms of friendship with thine enemies.
    Pardon me, Julius! Here wast thou bayed, brave hart.

Here didst thou fall, and here thy hunters stand   220
Signed in thy spoil, and crimsoned in thy lethe.
O world, thou wast the forest to this hart,
And this indeed, O world, the heart of thee.
How like a deer, strucken by many princes,
Dost thou here lie!

CASSIUS: Mark Antony —

ANTONY: Pardon me, Caius Cassius.
    The enemies of Caesar shall say this.
    Then, in a friend, it is cold modesty.

CASSIUS: I blame you not for praising Caesar so,   230
    But what compact mean you to have with us?
    Will you be pricked in number of our friends,
    Or shall we on, and not depend on you?

ANTONY: Therefore I took your hands, but was indeed,
    Swayed from the point, by looking down on Caesar.
    Friends am I with you all, and love you all,
    Upon this hope, that you shall give me reasons,
    Why, and wherein, Caesar was dangerous.

BRUTUS: Or else were this a savage spectacle.
    Our reasons are so full of good regard   240
    That were you Antony, the son of Caesar,
    You should be satisfied.

ANTONY: That's all I seek,
    And am moreover suitor, that I may
    Produce his body to the market-place,
    And in the pulpit, as becomes a friend,
    Speak in the order of his funeral.

BRUTUS: You shall, Mark Antony,

CASSIUS: Brutus, a word with you.

[Aside to Brutus.]

You know not what you do. Do not consent   250
That Antony speak in his funeral.
Know you how much the people may be moved
By that which he will utter?

BRUTUS: By your pardon,
    I will myself into the pulpit first,
    And show the reason of our Caesar's death.
    What Antony shall speak, I will protest
    He speaks by leave, and by permission,
    And that we are contented Caesar shall
    Have all true rites, and lawful ceremonies.   260
    It shall advantage more, than do us wrong.

221. *Signed ... spoil* – marked with the blood of your slaughter
221. *lethe* – river in Hades whose waters cause forgetfulness

229. *modesty* – moderation

231. *compact* – agreement; understanding
232. *pricked* – marked down
234. *Therefore* – for that reason

239. *Or else were* – if not, this would be

244. *suitor* – one who asks permission

247. *order* – ceremony

277. *tide of times* – course of history
283. *Domestic ... strife* – civil war
284. *cumber* – oppress; overwhelm
288. *quartered* – cut to pieces
289. *with custom* – by becoming accustomed
289. *fell* – cruel
290. *ranging for* – wandering in search of
291. *Ate* – Greek goddess of revenge and destruction

293. *Cry havoc* – This was an order that only kings could give. It instructed the army to pillage and slaughter with no mercy. Note that it is Caesar's spirit that Antony imagines gives the order.

293. *let slip* – unleash
295. *carrion men* – corpses

CASSIUS: I know not what may fall. I like it not.
BRUTUS: Mark Antony, here, take you Caesar's body.
  You shall not in your funeral speech blame us,
  But speak all good you can devise of Caesar,
  And say you do it by our permission.
  Else shall you not have any hand at all
  About his funeral. And you shall speak
  In the same pulpit whereto I am going,
  After my speech is ended.   270
ANTONY: Be it so.
  I do desire no more.
BRUTUS: Prepare the body then, and follow us.

Exeunt all but Antony.

ANTONY: O pardon me, thou bleeding piece of earth,
  That I am meek and gentle with these butchers!
  Thou art the ruins of the noblest man
  That ever lived in the tide of times.
  Woe to the hand that shed this costly blood!
  Over thy wounds, now do I prophesy,
  Which like dumb mouths do ope their ruby lips,   280
  To beg the voice and utterance of my tongue,
  A curse shall light upon the limbs of men.
  Domestic fury, and fierce civil strife,
  Shall cumber all the parts of Italy.
  Blood and destruction shall be so in use,
  And dreadful objects so familiar,
  That mothers shall but smile when they behold
  Their infants quartered with the hands of war.
  All pity choked with custom of fell deeds,
  And Caesar's spirit ranging for revenge,   290
  With Ate by his side, come hot from hell,
  Shall in these confines, with a monarch's voice,
  Cry havoc, and let slip the dogs of war,
  That this foul deed shall smell above the earth
  With carrion men, groaning for burial.

Enter Octavius' Servant.

  You serve Octavius Caesar, do you not?
SERVANT: I do, Mark Antony.
ANTONY: Caesar did write for him to come to Rome.

SERVANT: He did receive his letters, and is coming;
    And bid me say to you by word of mouth —   300
    O Caesar!
ANTONY: Thy heart is big. Get thee apart and weep.
    Passion I see, is catching, for mine eyes,
    Seeing those beads of sorrow stand in thine,
    Began to water. Is thy master coming?
SERVANT: He lies tonight within seven leagues of Rome.
ANTONY: Post back with speed,
    And tell him what hath chanced.
    Here is a mourning Rome, a dangerous Rome,
    No Rome of safety for Octavius yet.   310
    Hie hence, and tell him so. Yet, stay awhile.
    Thou shalt not back, till I have borne this corse
    Into the market-place. There shall I try
    In my oration, how the people take
    The cruel issue of these bloody men,
    According to the which, thou shalt discourse
    To young Octavius, of the state of things.
    Lend me your hand.

        Exeunt [with Caesar's body].

302. *big* – full of grief
303. *Passion* – sorrow

306. *seven leagues* – twenty-one miles or 34 km

310. *Rome* – perhaps a pun on "room"
313. *try* – test

315. *issue* – work

Act Three
Scene 2

Rome. The Forum.

Brutus addresses the Roman citizens and convinces them that, because of Caesar's ambition, his death was necessary to maintain freedom and the republic. Antony brings out Caesar's body, and by appealing to their emotions he convinces the citizens that Caesar was not ambitious and, therefore, the conspirators were not "honourable men." Antony produces Caesar's will, which names the Roman citizens as his heirs. The riotous mob begins to search out the conspirators. Word arrives that Octavius is in Rome and waiting to meet with Antony.

1. *Plebeians* – the commoners
4. *part* – divide

RELATED READING

I Saw Caesar Pass in Splendour – poem by Richard Woollatt (page 125)

11. *severally* – separately
13. *till the last* – until I finish speaking
17. *Censure* – judge
18. *senses* – common sense; reason

Enter Brutus and goes into the pulpit, and Cassius, with the Plebeians.

PLEBEIANS: We will be satisfied. Let us be satisfied.
BRUTUS: Then follow me, and give me audience friends.
 Cassius go you into the other street,
 And part the numbers.
 Those that will hear me speak, let 'em stay here.
 Those that will follow Cassius, go with him,
 And public reasons shall be rendered
 Of Caesar's death.
1. PLEBEIAN: I will hear Brutus speak.
2. PLEBEIAN: I will hear Cassius, and compare their reasons, 10
 When severally we hear them rendered.

[Exit Cassius, with some of the Plebeians.]

3. PLEBEIAN: The noble Brutus is ascended. Silence!
BRUTUS: Be patient till the last.
 Romans, countrymen, and lovers, hear me for my cause, and be silent, that you may hear. Believe me for mine honour, and have respect to mine honour, that you may believe. Censure me in your wisdom, and awake your senses, that you may the better judge. If there be any in this assembly, any dear friend of Caesar's, to him I say, that Brutus' love to Caesar, was no less than his. If then, 20 that friend demand why Brutus rose against Caesar, this is my answer: Not that I loved Caesar less, but that I loved Rome more. Had you rather Caesar were living and die all slaves, than that Caesar were dead, to live all

free men? As Caesar loved me, I weep for him; as he was fortunate, I rejoice at it; as he was valiant, I honour him. But, as he was ambitious, I slew him. There is tears for his love, joy for his fortune, honour for his valour, and death for his ambition. Who is here so base that would be a bondman? If any, speak, for him have I offended. **30** Who is here so rude, that would not be a Roman? If any, speak, for him have I offended. Who is here so vile that will not love his country? If any, speak, for him have I offended. I pause for a reply.

ALL: None, Brutus, none.

BRUTUS: Then none have I offended. I have done no more to Caesar than you shall do to Brutus. The question of his death is enrolled in the Capitol. His glory not extenuated, wherein he was worthy, nor his offences enforced, for which he suffered death. **40**

Enter Mark Antony, with Caesar's body.

Here comes his body, mourned by Mark Antony, who, though he had no hand in his death, shall receive the benefit of his dying, a place in the commonwealth, as which of you shall not? With this I depart, that, as I slew my best lover for the good of Rome, I have the same dagger for myself, when it shall please my country to need my death.

ALL: Live, Brutus! Live! Live!

1. PLEBEIAN: Bring him with triumph home unto his house.

2. PLEBEIAN: Give him a statue with his ancestors. **50**

3. PLEBEIAN: Let him be Caesar.

4. PLEBEIAN: Caesar's better parts
 Shall be crowned in Brutus.

1. PLEBEIAN: We'll bring him to his house,
 With shouts and clamours.

BRUTUS: My countrymen, —

2. PLEBEIAN: Peace, silence! Brutus speaks.

1. PLEBEIAN: Peace, ho!

BRUTUS: Good countrymen, let me depart alone,
 And, for my sake, stay here with Antony. **60**
 Do grace to Caesar's corpse, and grace his speech
 Tending to Caesar's glories, which Mark Antony,
 By our permission, is allowed to make.
 I do entreat you, not a man depart,
 Save I alone, till Antony have spoke.

Exit.

---

30. *bondman* – slave
31. *rude* – uncivilized

37. *question of* – reasons for
38. *enrolled* – recorded
39. *extenuated* – minimized
40. *enforced* – exaggerated

43. *commonwealth* – free republic

51. *Let him be Caesar* – An ironic twist, but consistent with Shakespeare's characterization of commoners (the plebeians) in this play and in several others. As a mob, they are unintelligent and fickle.

52. *parts* – qualities
55. *clamours* – noises

65. *Save* – except

69. *beholding* – obliged

83. *interred* – buried

1. PLEBEIAN: Stay, ho! And let us hear Mark Antony.
3. PLEBEIAN: Let him go up into the public chair.
    We'll hear him. Noble Antony, go up.
ANTONY: For Brutus' sake, I am beholding to you.

[Goes into the pulpit.]

4. PLEBEIAN: What does he say of Brutus?   70
3. PLEBEIAN: He says, for Brutus' sake
    He finds himself beholding to us all.
4. PLEBEIAN: 'Twere best he speak no harm of Brutus here.
1. PLEBEIAN: This Caesar was a tyrant.
3. PLEBEIAN: Nay, that's certain.
    We are blest that Rome is rid of him.
2. PLEBEIAN: Peace! let us hear what Antony can say.
ANTONY: You gentle Romans, —
PLEBEIANS: Peace, ho! Let us hear him.
ANTONY: Friends, Romans, countrymen, lend me your ears.   80
    I come to bury Caesar, not to praise him.
    The evil that men do lives after them,
    The good is oft interred with their bones.
    So let it be with Caesar. The noble Brutus
    Hath told you Caesar was ambitious.
    If it were so, it was a grievous fault,
    And grievously hath Caesar answered it.
    Here, under leave of Brutus, and the rest,

For Brutus is an honourable man,
So are they all, all honourable men,   90
Come I to speak in Caesar's funeral.
He was my friend, faithful, and just to me,
But Brutus says he was ambitious,
And Brutus is an honourable man.
He hath brought many captives home to Rome,
Whose ransoms did the general coffers fill.
Did this in Caesar seem ambitious?
When that the poor have cried, Caesar hath wept.
Ambition should be made of sterner stuff,
Yet Brutus says he was ambitious,   100
And Brutus is an honourable man.
You all did see that on the Lupercal,
I thrice presented him a kingly crown,
Which he did thrice refuse. Was this ambition?
Yet Brutus says, he was ambitious,
And sure he is an honourable man.
I speak not to disprove what Brutus spoke,
But here I am to speak what I do know.
You all did love him once, not without cause.
What cause withholds you then, to mourn for him?   110
O judgment, thou art fled to brutish beasts,
And men have lost their reason. Bear with me.
My heart is in the coffin there with Caesar,
And I must pause till it come back to me.

94. Antony is very careful when he begins his oration. The crowd is positive toward Brutus and will not tolerate anything negative being said about him. Antony will work at the crowd slowly and get them to realize that if Brutus was wrong in one thing (claiming that Caesar was ambitious), then Brutus could also have been wrong in killing Caesar.

111. *brutish* – perhaps a pun on Brutus' name

121. *dear abide it* – pay dearly for it

"*Paralipsis*, a mode of irony which works by disclaiming the very things the speaker wishes to emphasize, is one of [Antony's] most effective techniques. Repeating the word *wrong* six times within four lines, he insinuates that wrong has been done in the very process of denying that it has. Pretending to try to quiet the crowd, to dissuade them from *mutiny and rage*, he achieves his ends even as he disclaims them. His handling of the will ... similarly makes use of paralipsis; in enumerating all his reasons for withholding the will, he describes exactly the ways it will *inflame* them."
– Gayle Greene (b. 1943), American scholar and professor

135. *parchment* – document
136. *closet* – small private room
137. *commons* – common people
148. *meet* – appropriate

1. PLEBEIAN: Methinks there is much reason in his sayings.
2. PLEBEIAN: If thou consider rightly of the matter,
  Caesar has had great wrong.
3. PLEBEIAN: Has he masters? I fear there will a worse come in
  his place.
4. PLEBEIAN: Marked ye his words? He would not take the crown.
  Therefore 'tis certain he was not ambitious.   120
1. PLEBEIAN: If it be found so, some will dear abide it.
2. PLEBEIAN: Poor soul! His eyes are red as fire with weeping.
3. PLEBEIAN: There's not a nobler man in Rome than Antony.
4. PLEBEIAN: Now mark him, he begins again to speak.
ANTONY: But yesterday the word of Caesar might
  Have stood against the world. Now lies he there.
  And none so poor to do him reverence.
  O masters, if I were disposed to stir
  Your hearts and minds to mutiny and rage,
  I should do Brutus wrong, and Cassius wrong,   130
  Who, you all know, are honourable men.
  I will not do them wrong. I rather choose
  To wrong the dead, to wrong myself and you,
  Than I will wrong such honourable men.
  But here's a parchment, with the seal of Caesar.
  I found it in his closet, 'tis his will.
  Let but the commons hear this testament,
  Which pardon me, I do not mean to read,
  And they would go and kiss dead Caesar's wounds,
  And dip their napkins in his sacred blood,   140
  Yea, beg a hair of him for memory,
  And dying, mention it within their wills,
  Bequeathing it as a rich legacy
  Unto their issue.
4. PLEBEIAN: We'll hear the will. Read it, Mark Antony.
ALL: The will, the will! We will hear Caesar's will.
ANTONY: Have patience, gentle friends, I must not read it.
  It is not meet you know how Caesar loved you.
  You are not wood, you are not stones, but men,
  And, being men, bearing the will of Caesar,   150
  It will inflame you, it will make you mad.
  'Tis good you know not that you are his heirs,
  For if you should, O what would come of it?
4. PLEBEIAN: Read the will. We'll hear it Antony!
  You shall read us the will, Caesar's will.
ANTONY: Will you be patient? Will you stay awhile?
  I have overshot myself to tell you of it.

I fear I wrong the honourable men,
Whose daggers have stabbed Caesar. I do fear it.
4. PLEBEIAN: They were traitors. Honourable men!   160
ALL: The will! The testament!
2. PLEBEIAN: They were villains, murderers! The will! Read
the will.
ANTONY: You will compel me, then, to read the will?
Then make a ring about the corpse of Caesar,
And let me show you him that made the will.
Shall I descend? And will you give me leave?
SEVERAL PLEBEIANS: Come down.
2. PLEBEIAN: Descend.
3. PLEBEIAN: You shall have leave.

[Antony comes down.]

4. PLEBEIAN: A ring, stand round.   170
1. PLEBEIAN: Stand from the hearse, stand from the body.
2. PLEBEIAN: Room for Antony, most noble Antony.
ANTONY: Nay, press not so upon me. Stand far off.
SEVERAL PLEBEIANS: Stand back! Room! Bear back!
ANTONY: If you have tears, prepare to shed them now.
You all do know this mantle. I remember
The first time ever Caesar put it on.
'Twas on a summer's evening in his tent,
That day he overcame the Nervii.
Look, in this place ran Cassius' dagger through.   180
See what a rent the envious Casca made.
Through this, the well-beloved Brutus stabbed,
And as he plucked his cursed steel away,
Mark how the blood of Caesar followed it,
As rushing out of doors, to be resolved
If Brutus so unkindly knocked, or no,
For Brutus, as you know, was Caesar's angel.
Judge, O you gods, how dearly Caesar loved him!
This was the most unkindest cut of all.
For when the noble Caesar saw him stab,   190
Ingratitude, more strong than traitors' arms,
Quite vanquished him. Then burst his mighty heart,
And in his mantle, muffling up his face,
Even at the base of Pompey's statue,
Which all the while ran blood, great Caesar fell.
O what a fall was there, my countrymen!
Then I, and you, and all of us fell down,

171. *hearse* – funeral bier
179. *Nervii* – an important and especially fierce battle against a Gallic tribe, during which Caesar showed remarkable courage and strength

181. *envious* – malicious; jealous

189. Antony says that Brutus' cut "was the most unkindest cut of all." It was generally believed that Brutus was Caesar's illegitimate son. Caesar spared Brutus' life on more than one occasion, and this fuelled the speculation of Caesar's paternity.

193. *muffling* – covering

200. *dint* – effect
202. *vesture* – garment

RELATED READING

How to Report on What You've Seen or Read – poem by Frank Barone (page 126)

218. *private griefs* – personal grievances

222 – 223. Antony is being modest for rhetorical purposes.

"Is there any oration extant in which the topics are more skilfully selected for the minds and temper of the persons to whom it is spoken? Does it not by the most gentle gradations arrive at the point to which it was directed?"
– Elizabeth Montagu (1720 – 1800), English author and wit

Whilst bloody treason flourished over us.
O now you weep, and I perceive you feel
The dint of pity. These are gracious drops.   200
Kind souls, what weep you when you but behold
Our Caesar's vesture wounded? Look you here,
Here is himself, marred as you see with traitors.
1. PLEBEIAN: O piteous spectacle!
2. PLEBEIAN: O noble Caesar!
3. PLEBEIAN: O woeful day!
4. PLEBEIAN: O traitors, villains!
1. PLEBEIAN: O most bloody sight!
2. PLEBEIAN: We will be revenged.
ALL: Revenge! About! Seek! Burn! Fire! Kill! Slay!   210
      Let not a traitor live!
ANTONY: Stay, countrymen.
1. PLEBEIAN: Peace there! Hear the noble Antony.
2. PLEBEIAN: We'll hear him, we'll follow him, we'll die with him.
ANTONY: Good friends, sweet friends, let me not stir you up
      To such a sudden flood of mutiny.
      They that have done this deed are honourable.
      What private griefs they have, alas I know not,
      That made them do it. They are wise and honourable,
      And will no doubt with reasons answer you.   220
      I come not, friends, to steal away your hearts.
      I am no orator, as Brutus is,
      But, as you know me all, a plain blunt man,
      That love my friend, and that they know full well
      That gave me public leave to speak of him.
      For I have neither wit, nor words, nor worth,
      Action, nor utterance, nor the power of speech,
      To stir men's blood. I only speak right on.
      I tell you that which you yourselves do know,
      Show you sweet Caesar's wounds, poor poor dumb mouths, 230
      And bid them speak for me. But were I Brutus,
      And Brutus Antony, there were an Antony
      Would ruffle up your spirits, and put a tongue
      In every wound of Caesar, that should move
      The stones of Rome, to rise and mutiny.
ALL: We'll mutiny.
1. PLEBEIAN: We'll burn the house of Brutus.
3. PLEBEIAN: Away, then! Come, seek the conspirators.
ANTONY: Yet hear me countrymen. Yet hear me speak.
ALL: Peace ho! Hear Antony. Most noble Antony!   240
ANTONY: Why, friends, you go to do you know not what.
      Wherein hath Caesar thus deserved your loves?

Alas, you know not. I must tell you then.
You have forgot the will I told you of.

ALL: Most true. The will! Let's stay and hear the will.

ANTONY: Here is the will, and under Caesar's seal.
To every Roman citizen he gives,
To every several man, seventy-five drachmas.

2. PLEBEIAN: Most noble Caesar! We'll revenge his death.

3. PLEBEIAN: O royal Caesar!   250

ANTONY: Hear me with patience.

ALL: Peace, ho!

ANTONY: Moreover, he hath left you all his walks,
His private arbours, and new-planted orchards,
On this side Tiber; he hath left them you,
And to your heirs for ever, common pleasures,
To walk abroad, and recreate yourselves.
Here was a Caesar! When comes such another?

1. PLEBEIAN: Never, never. Come, away, away!
We'll burn his body in the holy place,   260
And with the brands fire the traitors' houses.
Take up the body.

2. PLEBEIAN: Go fetch fire.

3. PLEBEIAN: Pluck down benches.

4. PLEBEIAN: Pluck down forms, windows, anything.

Exeunt Plebeians [with the body].

ANTONY: Now let it work. Mischief, thou art afoot,
Take thou what course thou wilt!
How now, fellow!

Enter Servant.

SERVANT: Sir, Octavius is already come to Rome.

ANTONY: Where is he?   270

SERVANT: He and Lepidus are at Caesar's house.

ANTONY: And thither will I straight to visit him.
He comes upon a wish. Fortune is merry,
And in this mood will give us anything.

SERVANT: I heard him say, Brutus and Cassius
Are rid like madmen through the gates of Rome.

ANTONY: Belike they had some notice of the people,
How I had moved them. Bring me to Octavius.

Exeunt.

248. *seventy-five drachmas*
– Greek silver coins; in
today's currency, about $100

254. *arbours* – summer
retreats that were heavily
wooded

"Was Brutus a butcher or a
saint? Shakespeare's play
does not pass judgment,
but puts the question to
the crowd, who succes-
sively agree to both views,
and finally give the
decision to Antony."
– Dominique Goy-Blanquet,
French professor,
Université de Picardie

RELATED READING

*The Killing of Julius
Caesar "Localized"* –
fiction by Mark Twain
(page 127)

265. *windows* – i.e., shutters
273. *upon a wish* – at an
opportune time

An unsuspecting Cinna the Poet ventures outdoors and is accosted and killed by the mob because he bears the same name as one of the conspirators.

Act Three
Scene 3

Rome. A street.

Enter Cinna the Poet and after him the Plebeians.

1 – 2. Happy dreams were often interpreted as foreboding that something bad would happen.

3. *will* – desire

CINNA: I dreamt tonight, that I did feast with Caesar,
    And things unluckily charge my fantasy.
    I have no will to wander forth of doors,
    Yet something leads me forth.
1. PLEBEIAN: What is your name?
2. PLEBEIAN: Whither are you going?
3. PLEBEIAN: Where do you dwell?
4. PLEBEIAN: Are you a married man, or a bachelor?
2. PLEBEIAN: Answer every man directly.
1. PLEBEIAN: Ay, and briefly.   10
4. PLEBEIAN: Ay, and wisely.
3. PLEBEIAN: Ay, and truly, you were best.
CINNA: What is my name? Whither am I going? Where do I dwell? Am I a married man or a bachelor? Then, to answer every man, directly and briefly, wisely and truly: wisely I say, I am a bachelor.
2. PLEBEIAN: That's as much as to say, they are fools that marry. You'll bear me a bang for that, I fear. Proceed, directly.
CINNA: Directly I am going to Caesar's funeral.   20
1. PLEBEIAN: As a friend, or an enemy?
CINNA: As a friend.
2. PLEBEIAN: That matter is answered directly.
4. PLEBEIAN: For your dwelling, briefly.
CINNA: Briefly, I dwell by the Capitol.
3. PLEBEIAN: Your name sir, truly.

18. *bear ... bang* – will receive a hit

"The odd episode of Cinna the poet being lynched in error for Cinna the conspirator seems irrelevant, but in fact sums up a main theme of the play. There is everything in a name — for the ignorant and the irrational."
– Molly Maureen Mahood, British scholar and professor

CINNA: Truly, my name is Cinna.

1. PLEBEIAN: Tear him to pieces! He's a conspirator.

CINNA: I am Cinna the poet, I am Cinna the poet.

4. PLEBEIAN: Tear him for his bad verses, tear him for his   30
bad verses.

CINNA: I am not Cinna the conspirator.

4. PLEBEIAN: It is no matter, his name's Cinna. Pluck but his
name out of his heart, and turn him going.

3. PLEBEIAN: Tear him, tear him! Come, brands ho! Fire-
brands! To Brutus'! To Cassius'! Burn all! Some to
Decius' house, and some to Casca's. Some to Ligarius'.
Away, go!

Exeunt all the Plebeians
[dragging off Cinna the Poet].

ಌ ಌ ಌ

33 – 34. *Pluck ... going* –
"Pull but his name out of his
heart and then dispatch (kill)
him."

Act Three Considerations

ACT THREE Scene 1

▶ Imagine you are a newspaper or television reporter covering the assassination of Julius Caesar. Create the front page of a newspaper, or a videotape of a news report, that indicates the events leading up to, and including, the murder of Caesar. Include quotations from, or interviews with, some of the conspirators.

▶ We may feel that Caesar's fall is somewhat expected because of his hubris (excessive pride or arrogance). To what extent do you think the conspirators are also guilty of hubris after the assassination? Explain.

▶ In groups of two or more, compile by consensus a list of at least six statements that describe Mark Antony's character and motivation.

▶ After the conspirators leave, Antony foresees that all of Italy will suffer as a result of Caesar's murder. It is also clear that he sees himself as an instrument of vengeance. In your opinion, why would Antony feel justified in punishing more than just those who were immediately involved in the assassination of Caesar?

ACT THREE Scene 2

▶ Compare the speeches given by Brutus and Antony. How do they differ? What does Brutus assume about the citizens? What does Antony know about the citizens that enables him to manipulate them?

▶ If you were a speech coach or a professional speechwriter, what advice would you give Brutus to help him improve his oratorical skills?

▶ First individually, and then in small groups, write three statements supporting the view that Antony was acting as an "honourable man" during his funeral oration. Then write three statements that argue the opposite point of view. Which view do you agree with most? Why?

▶ Find and list as many examples of irony as you can in this scene. One form of irony that is especially effective here involves the use of words that echo lines from other scenes. When they are repeated in this scene, they are ironic. Find examples of these ironic echoes.

ACT THREE Scene 3

▶ What purpose is served by this short scene? What does it reveal about the mob?

▶ Think about experiences you have had with bullying. How do the plebeians behave like typical school-yard bullies? How has Cinna set himself up to be a victim?

Act Four
Scene 1

A house in Rome.

Octavius, Antony, and Lepidus, now in full control of Rome, meet to determine who shall be executed and who spared. Antony sends Lepidus on an errand and then discusses with Octavius how unworthy Lepidus is as a partner in their enterprise. They prepare to rally their resources against the formidable forces mustered by Brutus and Cassius.

Enter Antony, Octavius, and Lepidus.
[They sit at a table.]

ANTONY: These many, then, shall die. Their names are pricked.
OCTAVIUS: Your brother too must die. Consent you, Lepidus?
LEPIDUS: I do consent.
OCTAVIUS: Prick him down, Antony.
LEPIDUS: Upon condition Publius shall not live,
    Who is your sister's son, Mark Antony.
ANTONY: He shall not live. Look, with a spot I damn him.
    But, Lepidus, go you to Caesar's house.
    Fetch the will hither, and we shall determine
    How to cut off some charge in legacies.   10
LEPIDUS: What, shall I find you here?
OCTAVIUS: Or here, or at the Capitol.

Exit Lepidus.

ANTONY: This is a slight unmeritable man,
    Meet to be sent on errands. Is it fit
    The three-fold world divided, he should stand
    One of the three to share it?
OCTAVIUS: So you thought him,
    And took his voice who should be pricked to die,
    In our black sentence and proscription.
ANTONY: Octavius, I have seen more days than you,   20
    And though we lay these honours on this man,
    To ease ourselves of divers slanderous loads,
    He shall but bear them, as the ass bears gold,
    To groan and sweat under the business,

1. *pricked* – marked down on the list by pricking the paper with a pin

RELATED READING

Freedom, Farewell! – fiction by Phyllis Bentley (page 134)

7. *damn* – condemn
10. *cut ... legacies* – alter the will and thereby keep more of Caesar's inheritance for their own purposes
15. *three-fold world* – After Caesar's death, Octavius, Antony, and Lepidus formed the Second Triumvirate and assumed absolute power. Each ruled a third of the Roman world, which then consisted of Europe, North Africa, and Asia.
18. *voice* – vote
19. *proscription* – sentence of death
22. *divers ... loads* – burden of blame (by blaming Lepidus)

RELATED READING

A Conversation of Three – drama by G.W.F. Hegel (page 130)

Either led or driven, as we point the way.
And having brought our treasure where we will,
Then take we down his load, and turn him off,
Like to the empty ass, to shake his ears,
And graze in commons.

OCTAVIUS: You may do your will,   30
But he's a tried and valiant soldier.

ANTONY: So is my horse, Octavius, and for that
I do appoint him store of provender.
It is a creature that I teach to fight,
To wind, to stop, to run directly on.
His corporal motion governed by my spirit.
And, in some taste, is Lepidus but so.
He must be taught, and trained and bid go forth:
A barren-spirited fellow, one that feeds
On objects, arts and imitations,   40
Which, out of use and staled by other men,
Begin his fashion. Do not talk of him
But as a property. And now Octavius,
Listen great things. Brutus and Cassius
Are levying powers. We must straight make head.
Therefore let our alliance be combined,
Our best friends made, our means stretched
And let us presently go sit in council,
How covert matters may be best disclosed,
And open perils surest answered.   50

OCTAVIUS: Let us do so. For we are at the stake,
And bayed about with many enemies,
And some that smile have in their hearts, I fear
Millions of mischiefs.

Exeunt.

Act Four
Scene 2

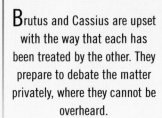

Brutus and Cassius are upset with the way that each has been treated by the other. They prepare to debate the matter privately, where they cannot be overheard.

A camp near Sardis. Before Brutus' tent.

Drum. Enter Brutus, Lucilius, [Lucius], and the Army. Titinius and Pindarus meet them.

BRUTUS: Stand, ho!

LUCILIUS: Give the word ho, and stand.

BRUTUS: What now, Lucilius, is Cassius near?

LUCILIUS: He is at hand, and Pindarus is come
　　To do you salutation from his master.

BRUTUS: He greets me well. Your master, Pindarus,
　　In his own change, or by ill officers,
　　Hath given me some worthy cause to wish
　　Things done, undone. But, if he be at hand,
　　I shall be satisfied.　　　　　　　　　　　10

PINDARUS: I do not doubt
　　But that my noble master will appear
　　Such as he is, full of regard and honour.

BRUTUS: He is not doubted. A word, Lucilius.
　　How he received you, let me be resolved.

LUCILIUS: With courtesy and with respect enough,
　　But not with such familiar instances,
　　Nor with such free and friendly conference,
　　As he hath used of old.

BRUTUS: Thou hast described　　　　　　　20
　　A hot friend cooling. Ever note, Lucilius,
　　When love begins to sicken and decay
　　It useth an enforced ceremony.
　　There are no tricks in plain and simple faith,
　　But hollow men, like horses hot at hand,
　　Make gallant show and promise of their mettle,

7. *change* – i.e., change in his feelings towards Brutus
7. *ill officers* – officers who have acted inappropriately

17. *familiar instances* – signs of familiarity (friendship)
18. *conference* – conversation
23. *enforced ceremony* – forced; unnatural courtesy
24. *faith* – friendship
25. *hollow* – insincere
25. *hot at hand* – fiery at first
26. *mettle* – spirit

27 – 29. *But ... trial* –
According to Brutus, such insincere men may show enthusiasm at first, but when it comes to the test they let their friends down. A *jade* is a worn-out horse.
30. *Sardis* – the capital of Lydia in Asia Minor. See map on page 10.
31. *horse in general* – cavalry
34. *gently* – politely; slowly

But when they should endure the bloody spur,
They fall their crests, and like deceitful jades,
Sink in the trial. Comes his army on?
LUCILIUS: They mean this night in Sardis to be quartered;   30
The greater part, the horse in general,
Are come with Cassius.
BRUTUS: Hark, he is arrived.

[Low march within.]

March gently on to meet him.

Enter Cassius and his powers.

CASSIUS: Stand, ho!
BRUTUS: Stand, ho! Speak the word along.
1. SOLDIER: Stand!
2. SOLDIER: Stand!
3. SOLDIER: Stand!
CASSIUS: Most noble brother, you have done me wrong.   40
BRUTUS: Judge me, you gods! Wrong I mine enemies?
And if not so, how should I wrong a brother?
CASSIUS: Brutus, this sober form of yours hides wrongs,
And when you do them —
BRUTUS: Cassius, be content.
Speak your griefs softly. I do know you well.
Before the eyes of both our armies here,
Which should perceive nothing but love from us,
Let us not wrangle. Bid them move away.
Then in my tent, Cassius, enlarge your griefs,   50
And I will give you audience.
CASSIUS: Pindarus,
Bid our commanders lead their charges off
A little from this ground.
BRUTUS: Lucius, do you the like, and let no man
Come to our tent till we have done our conference.
Let Lucilius and Titinius guard our door.

Exeunt. Brutus and Cassius remain.

43. *sober form* – calm exterior

50. *enlarge* – express at length

Act Four
Scene 3

Within Brutus' tent.

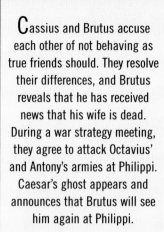

Cassius and Brutus accuse each other of not behaving as true friends should. They resolve their differences, and Brutus reveals that he has received news that his wife is dead. During a war strategy meeting, they agree to attack Octavius' and Antony's armies at Philippi. Caesar's ghost appears and announces that Brutus will see him again at Philippi.

CASSIUS: That you have wronged me doth appear in this:
　You have condemned and noted Lucius Pella
　For taking bribes here of the Sardians;
　Wherein my letters, praying on his side,
　Because I knew the man, were slighted off.
BRUTUS: You wronged yourself to write in such a case.
CASSIUS: In such a time as this, it is not meet
　That every nice offence should bear his comment.
BRUTUS: Let me tell you, Cassius, you yourself
　Are much condemned to have an itching palm,　　10
　To sell and mart your offices for gold
　To undeservers.
CASSIUS: I, an itching palm!
　You know that you are Brutus that speak this,
　Or, by the gods, this speech were else your last.
BRUTUS: The name of Cassius honours this corruption,
　And chastisement doth therefore hide his head.
CASSIUS: Chastisement!
BRUTUS: Remember March, the ides of March remember.
　Did not great Julius bleed for justice' sake?　　20
　What villain touched his body, that did stab,
　And not for justice? What, shall one of us,
　That struck the foremost man of all this world
　But for supporting robbers, shall we now
　Contaminate our fingers with base bribes,
　And sell the mighty space of our large honours
　For so much trash as may be grasped thus?
　I had rather be a dog, and bay the moon,
　Than such a Roman.

2. *noted* – punished by being publicly disgraced
5. *slighted off* – disregarded
8. *nice* – trivial
8. *bear his comment* – be subject to criticism
10. *itching palm* – hand ready to accept bribes
11. *mart your offices* – market lucrative positions of office
17. *chastisement ... head* – and, therefore, punishment does not occur
24. *supporting robbers* – This is a charge against Caesar not previously mentioned in the play. Shakespeare gets this detail directly from Plutarch.
26. *mighty ... honours* – great honours we can confer

"I had rather be a dog, and bay the moon"

32. *hedge me in* – place limitations on my authority
34. *conditions* – decisions

On the quarrel scene:
"I know no part of Shakespeare that more impresses on me the belief of his genius being super-human than this scene."
– Samuel Taylor Coleridge (1772 – 1834), English author, Romantic poet, and critic

43. *choler* – anger
44. *stares* – glares
46. *Fret* – rage
47. *choleric* – ill-tempered
48. *budge* – flinch
50. *testy humour* – irritable mood
51. *digest ... spleen* – swallow the poison of your anger
54. *waspish* – quick to take offence
57. *vaunting* – boasting
59. *learn of* – learn from

65. *moved* – angered
66. *tempted* – provoked

CASSIUS: Brutus, bait not me.   30
    I'll not endure it. You forget yourself,
    To hedge me in. I am a soldier, I,
    Older in practise, abler than yourself
    To make conditions.
BRUTUS: Go to. You are not, Cassius.
CASSIUS: I am.
BRUTUS: I say, you are not.
CASSIUS: Urge me no more, I shall forget myself.
    Have mind upon your health, tempt me no further.
BRUTUS: Away, slight man!   40
CASSIUS: Is it possible?
BRUTUS: Hear me, for I will speak.
    Must I give way, and room to your rash choler?
    Shall I be frighted, when a madman stares?
CASSIUS: O ye gods, ye gods! Must I endure all this?
BRUTUS: All this! Ay, more. Fret till your proud heart break.
    Go show your slaves how choleric you are,
    And make your bondmen tremble. Must I budge?
    Must I observe you? Must I stand and crouch
    Under your testy humour? By the gods,   50
    You shall digest the venom of your spleen,
    Though it do split you. For, from this day forth,
    I'll use you for my mirth, yea, for my laughter,
    When you are waspish.
CASSIUS: Is it come to this?
BRUTUS: You say you are a better soldier.
    Let it appear so. Make your vaunting true,
    And it shall please me well. For mine own part,
    I shall be glad to learn of noble men.
CASSIUS: You wrong me every way.   60
    You wrong me, Brutus.
    I said, an elder soldier, not a better.
    Did I say "better"?
BRUTUS: If you did, I care not.
CASSIUS: When Caesar lived, he durst not thus have moved me.
BRUTUS: Peace, peace! You durst not so have tempted him.
CASSIUS: I durst not!
BRUTUS: No.
CASSIUS: What? Durst not tempt him?
BRUTUS: For your life you durst not.   70
CASSIUS: Do not presume too much upon my love.
    I may do that I shall be sorry for.
BRUTUS: You have done that you should be sorry for.
    There is no terror, Cassius, in your threats,

For I am armed so strong in honesty,
That they pass by me as the idle wind,
Which I respect not. I did send to you
For certain sums of gold, which you denied me.
For I can raise no money by vile means.
By heaven, I had rather coin my heart, 80
And drop my blood for drachmas, than to wring
From the hard hands of peasants their vile trash
By any indirection. I did send
To you for gold to pay my legions,
Which you denied me. Was that done like Cassius?
Should I have answered Caius Cassius so?
When Marcus Brutus grows so covetous,
To lock such rascal counters from his friends,
Be ready gods with all your thunderbolts,
Dash him to pieces! 90

CASSIUS: I denied you not.

BRUTUS: You did.

CASSIUS: I did not. He was but a fool
That brought my answer back. Brutus hath rived my heart.
A friend should bear his friend's infirmities,
But Brutus makes mine greater than they are.

BRUTUS: I do not, till you practise them on me.

CASSIUS: You love me not.

BRUTUS: I do not like your faults.

CASSIUS: A friendly eye could never see such faults. 100

BRUTUS: A flatterer's would not, though they do appear
As huge as high Olympus.

CASSIUS: Come, Antony, and young Octavius, come,
Revenge yourselves alone on Cassius,
For Cassius is aweary of the world.
Hated by one he loves, braved by his brother,
Checked like a bondman, all his faults observed,
Set in a note-book, learned, and conned by rote,
To cast into my teeth. O, I could weep
My spirit from mine eyes! There is my dagger, 110
And here my naked breast. Within, a heart
Dearer than Pluto's mine, richer than gold.
If that thou be'st a Roman, take it forth.
I, that denied thee gold, will give my heart.
Strike, as thou didst at Caesar. For I know,
When thou didst hate him worst, thou lov'dst him better
Than ever thou lov'dst Cassius.

BRUTUS: Sheathe your dagger.
Be angry when you will, it shall have scope.

Pluto

75. *honesty* – integrity

82. *trash* – money
83. *indirection* – unjust methods

84. Roman soldiers did not work for and were not paid by the state. The soldiers were hired by individual generals. If the generals were unable to pay their salary, the soldiers would leave and join a general who could pay them.

88. *rascal counters* – trashy money
94. *rived* – broken
95. *bear* – put up with; tolerate

106. *braved* – defied
107. *Checked* – scolded
107. *observed* – scrutinized
108. *conned by rote* – memorized
112. *Dearer* – richer

112. *Pluto* – the Roman god of the underworld, the place where all riches originate; Plutus was the god of riches. These two names were often confused.

119. *scope* – free rein

Pluto

Act Four • Scene 3

Do what you will, dishonour shall be humour.   120
O Cassius, you are yoked with a lamb
That carries anger as the flint bears fire;
Who, much enforced, shows a hasty spark,
And straight is cold again.

CASSIUS: Hath Cassius lived
To be but mirth and laughter to his Brutus,
When grief and blood ill-tempered, vexeth him?

BRUTUS: When I spoke that, I was ill-tempered too.

CASSIUS: Do you confess so much? Give me your hand.

BRUTUS: And my heart too.   130

CASSIUS: O Brutus!

BRUTUS: What's the matter?

CASSIUS: Have not you love enough to bear with me,
When that rash humour which my mother gave me
Makes me forgetful?

BRUTUS: Yes, Cassius, and from henceforth,
When you are over-earnest with your Brutus,
He'll think your mother chides, and leave you so.

Enter a Poet [followed by Lucilius, Titinius, and Lucius].

POET: Let me go in to see the generals.
There is some grudge between 'em. 'Tis not meet   140
They be alone.

LUCILIUS: You shall not come to them.

POET: Nothing but death shall stay me.

CASSIUS: How now! What's the matter?

POET: For shame, you generals! What do you mean?
Love, and be friends, as two such men should be,
For I have seen more years, I'm sure, than ye.

CASSIUS: Ha, ha! How vilely doth this cynic rhyme!

BRUTUS: Get you hence, sirrah! Saucy fellow, hence!

CASSIUS: Bear with him, Brutus. 'Tis his fashion.   150

BRUTUS: I'll know his humour, when he knows his time.
What should the wars do with these jigging fools?
Companion, hence!

CASSIUS: Away, away, be gone!

Exit Poet.

BRUTUS: Lucilius and Titinius, bid the commanders
Prepare to lodge their companies tonight.

CASSIUS: And come yourselves, and bring Messala with you
Immediately to us.

[Exeunt Lucilius and Titinius.]

BRUTUS: Lucius, a bowl of wine!

[Exit Lucius.]

CASSIUS: I did not think you could have been so angry. 160
BRUTUS: O Cassius, I am sick of many griefs.
CASSIUS: Of your philosophy you make no use,
  If you give place to accidental evils.
BRUTUS: No man bears sorrow better. Portia is dead.
CASSIUS: Ha? Portia?
BRUTUS: She is dead.
CASSIUS: How 'scaped I killing when I crossed you so?
  O insupportable and touching loss!
  Upon what sickness?
BRUTUS: Impatient of my absence, 170
  And grief, that young Octavius with Mark Antony
  Have made themselves so strong. For with her death
  That tidings came. With this she fell distract,
  And, her attendants absent, swallowed fire.
CASSIUS: And died so?
BRUTUS: Even so.
CASSIUS: O ye immortal gods!

Enter Lucius with wine and tapers.

BRUTUS: Speak no more of her. Give me a bowl of wine.
  In this I bury all unkindness, Cassius.
CASSIUS: My heart is thirsty for that noble pledge. 180
  Fill, Lucius, till the wine overswell the cup.
  I cannot drink too much of Brutus' love.

[Exit Lucius.] Enter Titinius and Messala.

BRUTUS: Come in, Titinius.
  Welcome, good Messala.
  Now sit we close about this taper here,
  And call in question our necessities.
CASSIUS: *[To Brutus.]* Portia, art thou gone?
BRUTUS: No more, I pray you. —
  Messala, I have here received letters,
  That young Octavius and Mark Antony 190
  Come down upon us with a mighty power,
  Bending their expedition toward Philippi.
MESSALA: Myself have letters of the selfsame tenor.

162. *philosophy* – See note on Stoicism for Act One, Scene 2, line 48.

163. *place* – way; in

172 – 173. *For ... came* – Brutus alludes to the fact that he received a report with two pieces of information: Portia's death and news of Antony and Octavius' activities.

173 – 174. According to Plutarch, Portia "determining to kill herself ... took hot burning coals and cast them into her mouth so close, that she choked herself."

RELATED READING

The Bitterness of Love – poem by Dana K. Haight (page 140)

186. *call ... necessities* – discuss what needs to be done

87

Portia's death is dealt with twice in this scene. What needs to be explained is Brutus' surprised reaction when he hears it from Messala. Some editors argue that there is a compositional error here and that the second discussion should be deleted. It can also be argued, however, that Brutus hopes that, just as the two reports about the number of proscribed senators differ, so might news of his wife's death.

218. *art* – philosophy

220. *work alive* – task at hand
221. *Philippi* – (pronounced "phi-lip-eye") area in north-western Greece. See map on page 10.
221. *presently* – at once
227. *Doing ... offence* – weakening himself

231. *Do stand* – are loyal
232. *grudged us contribution* – been reluctant to contribute men and supplies
234. *make ... up* – increase in number

BRUTUS: With what addition?

MESSALA: That by proscription and bills of outlawry,
    Octavius, Antony, and Lepidus,
    Have put to death an hundred senators.

BRUTUS: Therein our letters do not well agree.
    Mine speak of seventy senators that died
    By their proscriptions, Cicero being one.   200

CASSIUS: Cicero one!

MESSALA: Cicero is dead, and by that order of proscription.
    Had you your letters from your wife, my lord?

BRUTUS: No, Messala.

MESSALA: Nor nothing in your letters writ of her?

BRUTUS: Nothing, Messala.

MESSALA: That, methinks, is strange.

BRUTUS: Why ask you?
    Hear you aught of her in yours?

MESSALA: No, my lord.   210

BRUTUS: Now, as you are a Roman, tell me true.

MESSALA: Then like a Roman, bear the truth I tell,
    For certain she is dead, and by strange manner.

BRUTUS: Why, farewell, Portia. We must die, Messala.
    With meditating that she must die once,
    I have the patience to endure it now.

MESSALA: Even so great men, great losses should endure.

CASSIUS: I have as much of this in art as you,
    But yet my nature could not bear it so.

BRUTUS: Well, to our work alive. What do you think   220
    Of marching to Philippi presently?

CASSIUS: I do not think it good.

BRUTUS: Your reason?

CASSIUS: This it is:
    'Tis better that the enemy seek us.
    So shall he waste his means, weary his soldiers,
    Doing himself offence, whilst we, lying still,
    Are full of rest, defense, and nimbleness.

BRUTUS: Good reasons must of force give place to better.
    The people 'twixt Philippi and this ground   230
    Do stand but in a forced affection,
    For they have grudged us contribution.
    The enemy, marching along by them,
    By them shall make a fuller number up,
    Come on refreshed, new-added, and encouraged.
    From which advantage shall we cut him off
    If at Philippi we do face him there,
    These people at our back.

CASSIUS: Hear me, good brother.

BRUTUS: Under your pardon. You must note beside,   240
That we have tried the utmost of our friends,
Our legions are brim-full, our cause is ripe.
The enemy increaseth every day;
We, at the height, are ready to decline.
There is a tide in the affairs of men,
Which, taken at the flood, leads on to fortune.
Omitted, all the voyage of their life
Is bound in shallows, and in miseries.
On such a full sea are we now afloat,
And we must take the current when it serves,   250
Or lose our ventures.

CASSIUS: Then, with your will, go on. We'll along
Ourselves, and meet them at Philippi.

BRUTUS: The deep of night is crept upon our talk,
And nature must obey necessity,
Which we will niggard with a little rest.
There is no more to say.

CASSIUS: No more. Good night.
Early tomorrow will we rise, and hence.

Enter Lucius [briefly].

BRUTUS: Lucius, my gown. Farewell, good Messala.   260
Good night, Titinius. Noble, noble Cassius,
Good night, and good repose.

CASSIUS: O my dear brother!
This was an ill beginning of the night.
Never come such division 'tween our souls!
Let it not, Brutus.

Enter Lucius, with the gown.

BRUTUS: Everything is well.

CASSIUS: Good night, my lord.

BRUTUS: Good night, good brother.

TITINIUS: } Good night, Lord Brutus.   270
MESSALA:

BRUTUS: Farewell, every one.

Exeunt [all but Brutus].

Give me the gown. Where is thy instrument?

LUCIUS: Here in the tent.

241. *tried* – tested

246. *flood* – high tide; opportune moment
247. *omitted* – missed

256. *niggard* – be stingy

"*Julius Caesar* is a story of politics. It tells of treachery and good intentions and the manipulations of mass emotions, and it rises to the final tragedy of civil war. Shakespeare has taken a page of Roman history and used it to show some disastrous truths about the nature of men and politics, and the result is a masterpiece."
– Marchete Chute (b. 1909), American literary historian

275. *over-watched* – exhausted

"Brutus' boy Lucius is very important. He is the repository for Brutus' frustrated paternal tenderness."
– Vera Lustig (b. 1942), Argentine scholar and professor

286. *otherwise … me* – change my mind

293. *an* – if

BRUTUS: What, thou speak'st drowsily?
    Poor knave, I blame thee not. Thou art over-watched.
    Call Claudio and some other of my men.
    I'll have them sleep on cushions in my tent.
LUCIUS: Varrus and Claudio!

Enter Varrus and Claudio.

VARRUS: Calls my lord?
BRUTUS: I pray you, sirs, lie in my tent and sleep.   280
    It may be I shall raise you by and by
    On business to my brother Cassius.
VARRUS: So please you, we will stand
    And watch your pleasure.
BRUTUS: I will not have it so. Lie down, good sirs.
    It may be I shall otherwise bethink me.

[Varrus and Claudio lie down.]

    Look, Lucius, here's the book I sought for so.
    I put it in the pocket of my gown.
LUCIUS: I was sure your lordship did not give it me.
BRUTUS: Bear with me good boy, I am much forgetful.   290
    Canst thou hold up thy heavy eyes awhile,
    And touch thy instrument a strain or two?
LUCIUS: Ay, my lord, an it please you.

BRUTUS: It does, my boy.
    I trouble thee too much, but thou art willing.
LUCIUS: It is my duty, sir.
BRUTUS: I should not urge thy duty past thy might.
    I know young bloods look for a time of rest.
LUCIUS: I have slept, my lord, already.
BRUTUS: It was well done, and thou shalt sleep again.   300
    I will not hold thee long. If I do live,
    I will be good to thee.

Music, and a song.

This is a sleepy tune. O murderous slumber!
Layest thou thy leaden mace upon my boy,
That plays thee music? Gentle knave, good night.
I will not do thee so much wrong to wake thee.
If thou dost nod, thou break'st thy instrument.
I'll take it from thee, and, good boy, good night.
Let me see, let me see. Is not the leaf turned down
Where I left reading? Here it is, I think.   310

Enter the Ghost of Caesar.

How ill this taper burns! Ha! Who comes here?
I think it is the weakness of mine eyes
That shapes this monstrous apparition.

304. *Layest ... mace* – a double allusion; both bailiffs and death would touch upon the shoulder with a mace (staff of office) or wand those whom they came for. *Leaden* means simply "heavy" in this context.

"[Shakespeare] shows great judgment in taking various opportunities to display the softness and gentleness of Brutus: the little circumstance of his forbearing to awaken [Lucius] is very beautiful; for one cannot conceive, that he whose tender humanity respected the slumber of his boy Lucius, would from malice or cruelty, have cut short the important and illustrious course of Caesar's life."
– Elizabeth Montagu (1720 – 1800), English author and wit

Act Four • Scene 3

316. *stare* – stand on end

> "[What] has been haunting Brutus throughout the scene finally takes form — in the ghost. The ghost 'embodies' (if such a word be permitted) that guilt, unconscious yet virulent, which has been torturing and driving Brutus."
> – Elias Schwartz (b. 1923), American professor

> "Brutus is concerned about the morale of his men. Thus three times in the course of one scene ... does Shakespeare show Brutus concealing his private distress to protect the morale of his army: they shall know nothing of his differences with Cassius, ... nor of his wife's suicide and the barbaric cruelty of the Triumvirate, nor of the ominous visitation of dead Caesar's ghost."
> – Warren D. Smith (b. 1911), American professor, University of Rhode Island

346. *betimes* – early

It comes upon me. Art thou any thing?
Art thou some god, some angel, or some devil,
That makest my blood cold and my hair to stare?
Speak to me, what thou art.
GHOST: Thy evil spirit, Brutus.
BRUTUS: Why comest thou?
GHOST: To tell thee thou shalt see me at Philippi.   320
BRUTUS: Well, then I shall see thee again?
GHOST: Ay, at Philippi.
BRUTUS: Why, I will see thee at Philippi then.

[Exit Ghost.]

Now I have taken heart, thou vanishest.
Ill spirit, I would hold more talk with thee.
Boy, Lucius! Varrus! Claudio! Sirs, awake!
Claudio!
LUCIUS: The strings, my lord, are false.
BRUTUS: He thinks he still is at his instrument.
Lucius, awake!   330
LUCIUS: My lord?
BRUTUS: Didst thou dream, Lucius, that thou so criedst out?
LUCIUS: My lord, I do not know that I did cry.
BRUTUS: Yes that thou didst. Didst see anything?
LUCIUS: Nothing, my lord.
BRUTUS: Sleep again, Lucius. Sirrah Claudio! Fellow,
Thou. Awake!
VARRUS: My lord?
CLAUDIO: My lord?
BRUTUS: Why did you so cry out sirs, in your sleep?   340
VARRUS:
CLAUDIO: } Did we, my lord?
BRUTUS: Ay. Saw you anything?
VARRUS: No, my lord, I saw nothing.
CLAUDIO: Nor I, my lord.
BRUTUS: Go, and commend me to my brother Cassius.
Bid him set on his powers betimes before,
And we will follow.
VARRUS:
CLAUDIO: } It shall be done, my lord.

Exeunt.

ଝ ଝ ଝ

Act Four Considerations

ACT FOUR **Scene 1**

▶ In what way is this scene ironic? Imagine you are Brutus and that you have just heard of the proscription of one hundred senators. Write a letter to Antony and Octavius telling them what you think of their actions. Mention the irony in the situation.

▶ What new character traits does Antony reveal in this scene? To what extent do you think Antony is beginning to take on the role of a villain?

▶ In this scene we get our first good look at Octavius. He will in time inherit the power and prestige that should have been Caesar's. Record your first impressions of Octavius. What traits introduced in this scene suggest that he may be worthy to follow in Caesar's footsteps?

ACT FOUR **Scenes 2 and 3**

▶ In what ways are Scenes 2 and 3 similar to Scene 1 in this Act? How are they different? You may wish to consider the relationship between the two sets of allies and the motivations for their actions.

▶ How does Cassius in these two scenes differ from Cassius in Act One?

▶ Whose side would you take in the argument between Cassius and Brutus? Why?

▶ If you were a director, how would you film or stage the ghost scene? Remember that one possible interpretation of the ghost is that he is not real, but rather an embodiment of Brutus' guilty conscience.

Act Five
Scene 1

The plains of Philippi.

Before the final battle on the plains of Philippi, Octavius and Antony exchange insults with Brutus and Cassius. They each withdraw and prepare to fight. Cassius expresses pessimism about the day's outcome to Messala, and, before leaving to join his forces, Cassius bids a final farewell to Brutus.

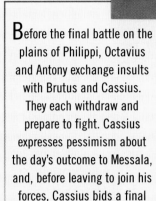

Enter Octavius, Antony, and their Army.

OCTAVIUS: Now, Antony, our hopes are answered.
 You said the enemy would not come down,
 But keep the hills and upper regions.
 It proves not so. Their battles are at hand.
 They mean to warn us at Philippi here,
 Answering before we do demand of them.
ANTONY: Tut, I am in their bosoms, and I know
 Wherefore they do it. They could be content
 To visit other places, and come down
 With fearful bravery, thinking by this face   10
 To fasten in our thoughts that they have courage;
 But 'tis not so.

Enter a Messenger.

MESSENGER: Prepare you, generals.
 The enemy comes on in gallant show.
 Their bloody sign of battle is hung out,
 And something to be done immediately.
ANTONY: Octavius, lead your battle softly on,
 Upon the left hand of the even field.
OCTAVIUS: Upon the right hand I. Keep thou the left.
ANTONY: Why do you cross me in this exigent?   20
OCTAVIUS: I do not cross you. But I will do so.

March.

Drum. Enter Brutus, Cassius, and their Army;
[Lucilius, Titinius, Messala, and others].

4. *battles* – forces
5. *warn* – challenge
6. *Answering* – responding (to our threat)
7. *in their bosoms* – know what they are thinking
9. *visit* – take safety in
9. *come down* – attack
10. *face* – outward show

15. *bloody sign* – red flag, signifying immediate engagement in battle

18 – 20. To the Romans, taking the right-hand side of the field of battle showed superiority.

20. *exigent* – crisis

95

22. *parley* – a conference

30. *bad strokes* – a reference to either Octavius' inexperience as a soldier or the strokes of the pen that condemned so many Romans after Caesar's death

35. *posture* – nature and effect
36 – 37. A reference to the effects of Antony's funeral oration. *Hybla* is an area in Sicily noted for its excellent honey.

42 – 43. According to Plutarch, the conspirators in their frenzy to kill Caesar "did hurt themselves striking one body with so many blows."

44. *showed your teeth* – grinned
49. *thank yourself* – you have yourself to thank
51. *ruled* – had his way (in the decision not to kill Antony as well as Caesar). Notice that Brutus remains silent during this particular exchange.
52. *cause* – matter at hand
55. *goes up* – is put back in its sheath
56. *three and thirty* – perhaps a misprint. Plutarch mentions three and twenty.
57. *another Caesar* – i.e., Octavius
63. *strain* – family
65 – 66. *peevish ... reveller* – insults directed at Octavius, who was only twenty-one, and Antony, who was a frequenter of plays and wild parties

BRUTUS: They stand, and would have parley.
CASSIUS: Stand fast, Titinius. We must out and talk.
OCTAVIUS: Mark Antony, shall we give sign of battle?
ANTONY: No, Caesar, we will answer on their charge.
    Make forth, the generals would have some words.
OCTAVIUS: Stir not until the signal.
BRUTUS: Words before blows. Is it so, countrymen?
OCTAVIUS: Not that we love words better, as you do.
BRUTUS: Good words are better than bad strokes, Octavius.   30
ANTONY: In your bad strokes, Brutus, you give good words.
    Witness the hole you made in Caesar's heart,
    Crying "Long live! Hail, Caesar!"
CASSIUS: Antony,
    The posture of your blows are yet unknown,
    But for your words, they rob the Hybla bees,
    And leave them honeyless.
ANTONY: Not stingless too.
BRUTUS: O, yes, and soundless too,
    For you have stolen their buzzing, Antony,   40
    And very wisely threat before you sting.
ANTONY: Villains, you did not so when your vile daggers
    Hacked one another in the sides of Caesar.
    You showed your teeth like apes,
    And fawned like hounds,
    And bowed like bondmen, kissing Caesar's feet,
    Whilst damned Casca, like a cur, behind
    Struck Caesar on the neck. O you flatterers!
CASSIUS: Flatterers! Now Brutus, thank yourself.
    This tongue had not offended so today,   50
    If Cassius might have ruled.
OCTAVIUS: Come, come, the cause. If arguing make us sweat,
    The proof of it will turn to redder drops.
    Look, I draw a sword against conspirators.
    When think you that the sword goes up again?
    Never, till Caesar's three and thirty wounds
    Be well avenged; or till another Caesar
    Have added slaughter to the sword of traitors.
BRUTUS: Caesar, thou canst not die by traitors' hands,
    Unless thou bringest them with thee.   60
OCTAVIUS: So I hope.
    I was not born to die on Brutus' sword.
BRUTUS: O, if thou wert the noblest of thy strain,
    Young man, thou couldst not die more honourable.
CASSIUS: A peevish schoolboy, worthless of such honour,
    Joined with a masker and a reveller!

ANTONY: Old Cassius still!

OCTAVIUS: Come Antony, away!
     Defiance, traitors, hurl we in your teeth.
     If you dare fight today, come to the field;   70
     If not, when you have stomachs.

Exeunt Octavius, Antony, and Army.

CASSIUS: Why, now, blow wind, swell billow
     And swim bark!
     The storm is up, and all is on the hazard.

BRUTUS: Ho Lucilius, hark, a word with you.

Lucilius and Messala stand forth.

LUCILIUS: My lord?

CASSIUS: Messala!

MESSALA: What says my general?

CASSIUS: Messala, this is my birthday, as this very day
     Was Cassius born. Give me thy hand, Messala.   80
     Be thou my witness that against my will,
     As Pompey was, am I compelled to set
     Upon one battle all our liberties.
     You know, that I held Epicurus strong,
     And his opinion. Now I change my mind,
     And partly credit things that do presage.
     Coming from Sardis, on our former ensign
     Two mighty eagles fell, and there they perched,
     Gorging and feeding from our soldiers' hands,
     Who to Philippi here consorted us.   90
     This morning are they fled away and gone,
     And in their steads, do ravens, crows and kites,
     Fly over our heads and downward look on us
     As we were sickly prey. Their shadows seem
     A canopy most fatal, under which
     Our army lies, ready to give up the ghost.

MESSALA: Believe not so.

CASSIUS: I but believe it partly,
     For I am fresh of spirit, and resolved
     To meet all perils very constantly.   100

BRUTUS: Even so, Lucilius.

CASSIUS: Now, most noble Brutus,
     The gods today stand friendly, that we may,
     Lovers in peace, lead on our days to age.
     But since the affairs of men rest still incertain,

71. *stomachs* – courage; guts

72. *billow* – waves

73. *bark* – ship

74. *on the hazard* – up for grabs; at stake

84 – 96. Epicurus taught that the gods were disinterested in the lives of human beings, and, therefore, that signs and omens mean nothing. Earlier in the play, the night before Caesar's murder, Cassius showed defiance towards the heavens. But in the end, when he sees crows and ravens displace the eagles flying with his army, Cassius begins to reject Epicurus' teaching about the import of "things that do presage."

86. *presage* – forebode

87. *ensign* – flag or standard

ensign

90. *consorted* – accompanied

92. *kites* – scavenger hawks

95. *most fatal* – foreboding death

99. *fresh of spirit* – optimistic

100. *constantly* – without hesitation

104. *Lovers ... age* – friends during peaceful times may live to see old age

Act Five • Scene 1

106. *reason* – consider

115. *time* – natural end
116. *stay ... of* – await the
fate ordained by

110 – 124. Brutus at first
claims that he will act
according to his philosophy of
Stoicism, which disapproves of
suicide. His father-in-law,
Cato the Elder, killed himself
rather than be captured by
Caesar. Brutus did not approve
of his decision. In his next
speech, however, he promises
that he will kill himself rather
than be taken prisoner. The
contradiction may be resolved
by thinking of the first position
as being spoken by Brutus the
Stoic, and the second by
Brutus the proud Roman
soldier.

136. *sufficeth* – is enough to
know

Let's reason with the worst that may befall.
If we do lose this battle, then is this
The very last time we shall speak together.
What are you then determined to do?

BRUTUS: Even by the rule of that philosophy   110
By which I did blame Cato for the death
Which he did give himself, I know not how,
But I do find it cowardly and vile,
For fear of what might fall, so to prevent
The time of life, arming myself with patience
To stay the providence of some high powers
That govern us below.

CASSIUS: Then, if we lose this battle,
You are contented to be led in triumph
Thorough the streets of Rome?   120

BRUTUS: No, Cassius, no.
Think not thou noble Roman,
That ever Brutus will go bound to Rome.
He bears too great a mind. But this same day
Must end that work the ides of March begun.
And whether we shall meet again, I know not.
Therefore our everlasting farewell take.
For ever, and for ever, farewell Cassius!
If we do meet again, why we shall smile;
If not, why then this parting was well made.   130

CASSIUS: For ever, and for ever, farewell Brutus!
If we do meet again, we'll smile indeed;
If not, 'tis true this parting was well made.

BRUTUS: Why then, lead on. O that a man might know
The end of this day's business, ere it come!
But it sufficeth that the day will end,
And then the end is known. Come, ho! Away!

Exeunt.

Act Five
Scene 2

Philippi. The field of battle.

Alarum. Enter Brutus and Messala.

BRUTUS: Ride, ride Messala, ride and give these bills
Unto the legions on the other side.

Loud alarum.

Let them set on at once, for I perceive
But cold demeanour in Octavius' wing,
And sudden push gives them the overthrow.
Ride, ride Messala. Let them all come down.

Exeunt.

Brutus sends Messala with orders for Cassius. The army of Octavius is losing badly and a new attack is sure to defeat them.

1. *bills* – orders

3. *set on* – attack
4. *cold demeanour* – lack of spirit or resolve
5. *sudden ... overthrow* – quick attack will defeat them

99

Act Five
Scene 3

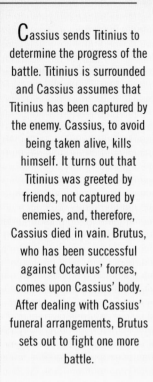

Cassius sends Titinius to determine the progress of the battle. Titinius is surrounded and Cassius assumes that Titinius has been captured by the enemy. Cassius, to avoid being taken alive, kills himself. It turns out that Titinius was greeted by friends, not captured by enemies, and, therefore, Cassius died in vain. Brutus, who has been successful against Octavius' forces, comes upon Cassius' body. After dealing with Cassius' funeral arrangements, Brutus sets out to fight one more battle.

1. *villains* – some of Cassius' soldiers
3. *ensign* – standard bearer
7. *spoil* – looting the dead bodies

Philippi. Another part of the field.

Alarums. Enter Cassius and Titinius.

CASSIUS: O look, Titinius, look, the villains fly!
    Myself have to mine own turned enemy.
    This ensign here of mine was turning back.
    I slew the coward, and did take it from him.
TITINIUS: O Cassius, Brutus gave the word too early,
    Who, having some advantage on Octavius,
    Took it too eagerly. His soldiers fell to spoil,
    Whilst we by Antony are all enclosed.

Enter Pindarus.

PINDARUS: Fly further off, my lord, fly further off!
    Mark Antony is in your tents, my lord.   10
    Fly, therefore, noble Cassius, fly far off!
CASSIUS: This hill is far enough. Look, look Titinius!
    Are those my tents where I perceive the fire?
TITINIUS: They are, my lord.
CASSIUS: Titinius, if thou lovest me,
    Mount thou my horse, and hide thy spurs in him,
    Till he have brought thee up to yonder troops,
    And here again, that I may rest assured
    Whether yond troops are friend or enemy.
TITINIUS: I will be here again, even with a thought.   20

Exit.

CASSIUS: Go, Pindarus, get higher on that hill.
　　　My sight was ever thick. Regard Titinius,
　　　And tell me what thou not'st about the field.

[Pindarus ascends the hill.]

　　　This day I breathed first, time is come round,
　　　And where I did begin, there shall I end.
　　　My life is run his compass. Sirrah, what news?
PINDARUS: *[Above.]* O my lord!
CASSIUS: What news?
PINDARUS: *[Above.]* Titinius is enclosed round about
　　　With horsemen, that make to him on the spur,　　　30
　　　Yet he spurs on. Now they are almost on him.
　　　Now Titinius. Now some light. O, he lights too.
　　　He's taken.

Shout.

　　　And, hark! They shout for joy.
CASSIUS: Come down, behold no more.
　　　O, coward that I am, to live so long,
　　　To see my best friend taken before my face!

Enter Pindarus [from above].

　　　Come hither sirrah. In Parthia did I take thee prisoner,
　　　And then I swore thee, saving of thy life,
　　　That whatsoever I did bid thee do,　　　40
　　　Thou shouldst attempt it. Come now, keep thine oath.
　　　Now be a freeman, and with this good sword,
　　　That ran through Caesar's bowels, search this bosom.
　　　Stand not to answer. Here, take thou the hilts,
　　　And, when my face is covered, as 'tis now,
　　　Guide thou the sword.

[Pindarus stabs him.]

　　　　　Caesar, thou art revenged,
　　　Even with the sword that killed thee.

[Dies.]

24. *breathed first* – i.e., at his birth
26. *compass* – course
30. *on the spur* – in a rush
32. *light* – alight; dismount

38. *Parthia* – area once known as Persia and now known as Iran.

43. *search* – penetrate

Act Five • Scene 3

54. *change* – an exchange (of fortune)

72. *melancholy's child* – one of the products of melancholy would be fear of unreal dangers and pessimism
73. *apt* – too willing to be fooled

81. *envenomed* – poisoned

RELATED READING

Dream and Interpretation:
Julius Caesar – literary essay by Marjorie B. Garber (page 143)

PINDARUS: So, I am free,
    Yet would not so have been,   50
    Durst I have done my will. O Cassius,
    Far from this country Pindarus shall run,
    Where never Roman shall take note of him.

    [Exit Pindarus.] Enter Titinius and Messala.

MESSALA: It is but change, Titinius, for Octavius
    Is overthrown by noble Brutus' power,
    As Cassius' legions are by Antony.
TITINIUS: These tidings will well comfort Cassius.
MESSALA: Where did you leave him?
TITINIUS: All disconsolate,
    With Pindarus his bondman, on this hill.   60
MESSALA: Is not that he that lies upon the ground?
TITINIUS: He lies not like the living. O my heart!
MESSALA: Is not that he?
TITINIUS: No, this was he, Messala,
    But Cassius is no more. O setting sun,
    As in thy red rays thou dost sink to night,
    So in his red blood Cassius' day is set.
    The sun of Rome is set! Our day is gone.
    Clouds, dews, and dangers come. Our deeds are done!
    Mistrust of my success hath done this deed.   70
MESSALA: Mistrust of good success hath done this deed.
    O hateful error, melancholy's child,
    Why dost thou show to the apt thoughts of men
    The things that are not? O error, soon conceived,
    Thou never comest unto a happy birth,
    But kill'st the mother that engendered thee.
TITINIUS: What Pindarus! Where art thou, Pindarus?
MESSALA: Seek him Titinius, whilst I go to meet
    The noble Brutus, thrusting this report
    Into his ears. I may say thrusting it,   80
    For piercing steel, and darts envenomed
    Shall be as welcome to the ears of Brutus
    As tidings of this sight.
TITINIUS: Hie you, Messala,
    And I will seek for Pindarus the while.

    [Exit Messala.]

Why didst thou send me forth, brave Cassius?
Did I not meet thy friends, and did not they

Put on my brows this wreath of victory,
And bid me give it thee? Didst thou not hear their shouts?
Alas, thou hast misconstrued everything.   90
But hold thee, take this garland on thy brow.
Thy Brutus bid me give it thee, and I
Will do his bidding. Brutus, come apace,
And see how I regarded Caius Cassius.
By your leave, gods. This is a Roman's part.
Come, Cassius' sword, and find Titinius' heart.

[Kills himself.]

Alarum. Enter Brutus, Messala, young Cato,
Strato, Volumnius, and Lucilius.

BRUTUS: Where, where Messala, doth his body lie?
MESSALA: Lo yonder, and Titinius mourning it.
BRUTUS: Titinius' face is upward.
CATO: He is slain.   100
BRUTUS: O Julius Caesar, thou art mighty yet!
    Thy spirit walks abroad, and turns our swords
    In our own proper entrails.

Low alarums.

CATO: Brave Titinius!
    Look, where he have not crowned dead Cassius.
BRUTUS: Are yet two Romans living such as these?
    The last of all the Romans, fare thee well!
    It is impossible that ever Rome
    Should breed thy fellow. Friends, I owe more tears
    To this dead man than you shall see me pay.   110
    I shall find time, Cassius, I shall find time.
    Come therefore, and to Thasos send his body.
    His funerals shall not be in our camp,
    Lest it discomfort us. Lucilius, come,
    And come, young Cato. Let us to the field.
    Labeo and Flavius, set our battles on.
    'Tis three o'clock, and Romans, yet ere night
    We shall try fortune in a second fight.

Exeunt.

91. *garland* – wreath of victory

wreath of victory

93. *apace* – quickly

95. *By your leave* – with your permission
95. *part* – duty

RELATED READING

Bugbears by Moonlight – literary essay by H.N. Hudson (page 141)

"[Brutus] comes to realize that in uplifting the sacred cause of freedom, in protecting the republic from the violence of tyranny and dictatorship, he has broken the equally binding law of humanity."
– Anne Paolucci, American playwright, poet, and scholar

109. *fellow* – match; equal
112. *Thasos* – island near Philippi off the coast of Thrace

114. *Lest it discomfort us* – Brutus avoids a situation that would serve to demoralize his men. See note on page 92.

116. *battles* – armies

Act Five • Scene 3

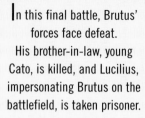

In this final battle, Brutus' forces face defeat. His brother-in-law, young Cato, is killed, and Lucilius, impersonating Brutus on the battlefield, is taken prisoner.

Act Five
Scene 4

Philippi. Another part of the field.

Alarum. Enter Brutus, Messala, Cato, Lucilius, and Flavius.

BRUTUS: Yet, countrymen, O, yet hold up your heads!

[Exit Brutus.]

2. *bastard* – untrue son (of Rome)

CATO: What bastard doth not? Who will go with me?
I will proclaim my name about the field.
I am the son of Marcus Cato, ho!
A foe to tyrants, and my country's friend.
I am the son of Marcus Cato, ho!

Enter Soldiers, and fight.

7. *And I am Brutus* – It was common practice in large battles, if a king or general was directly involved, to have a number of soldiers impersonate the leader to divert attention away from him.

LUCILIUS: And I am Brutus, Marcus Brutus, I!
Brutus, my country's friend. Know me for Brutus!

[In the fighting, Young Cato is killed.]

O young and noble Cato, art thou down?
Why now thou diest, as bravely as Titinius,   10
And mayst be honoured, being Cato's son.
1. SOLDIER: Yield, or thou diest.
LUCILIUS: Only I yield to die.
There is so much that thou wilt kill me straight.

14. *There ... straight* – You can profit greatly by killing me immediately.

[Offering money.]

Kill Brutus, and be honoured in his death.

1. SOLDIER: We must not. A noble prisoner!

Enter Antony.

2. SOLDIER: Room, ho! Tell Antony, Brutus is taken.
1. SOLDIER: I'll tell the news. Here comes the general.
    Brutus is taken, Brutus is taken, my lord.
ANTONY: Where is he?   20
LUCILIUS: Safe, Antony. Brutus is safe enough.
    I dare assure thee, that no enemy
    Shall ever take alive the noble Brutus.
    The gods defend him from so great a shame!
    When you do find him, or alive or dead,
    He will be found like Brutus, like himself.
ANTONY: This is not Brutus, friend, but, I assure you,
    A prize no less in worth. Keep this man safe.
    Give him all kindness. I had rather have
    Such men my friends than enemies. Go on,   30
    And see whether Brutus be alive or dead.
    And bring us word, unto Octavius' tent
    How everything is chanced.

Exeunt.

25. *or ... or* – either ... or
26. *like himself* – i.e., noble to the end

Act Five
Scene 5

Philippi. Another part of the field.

1. *poor remains* – what is left

2. *Statilius* – According to Plutarch, Statilius volunteered to make his way through the enemy to scout out Brutus' camp. He sent the signal (the torch-light) that all was well, but he was killed on his way back to Brutus.

"The main issue of the play is not the conspirators' fate but the future of Rome, of liberty, of the human race, to which their fate is incidental. Though Brutus is a tragic hero whom we pity as a man, the heart of his tragedy is the defeat of his cause. His death is but a symbol of a greater disaster, the death of liberty."
– J. Dover Wilson (1881 – 1969), British scholar

Enter Brutus, Dardanius, Clitus, Strato, and Volumnius.

BRUTUS: Come poor remains of friends, rest on this rock.
CLITUS: Statilius showed the torch-light, but my lord,
    He came not back. He is or taken, or slain.
BRUTUS: Sit thee down, Clitus. Slaying is the word;
    It is a deed in fashion. Hark thee, Clitus.

[Whispers.]

CLITUS: What I, my lord? No, not for all the world.
BRUTUS: Peace then! No words.
CLITUS: I'll rather kill myself.
BRUTUS: Hark thee, Dardanius.

[Whispers.]

DARDANIUS: Shall I do such a deed?   10
CLITUS: O Dardanius!
DARDANIUS: O Clitus!
CLITUS: What ill request did Brutus make to thee?
DARDANIUS: To kill him, Clitus. Look, he meditates.
CLITUS: Now is that noble vessel full of grief,
    That it runs over even at his eyes.
BRUTUS: Come hither, good Volumnius. List a word.
VOLUMNIUS: What says my lord?
BRUTUS: Why, this, Volumnius:
    The ghost of Caesar hath appeared to me   20

Two several times by night, at Sardis once,
And this last night, here in Philippi fields.
I know my hour is come.
VOLUMNIUS: Not so, my lord.
BRUTUS: Nay, I am sure it is, Volumnius.
Thou seest the world, Volumnius, how it goes.
Our enemies have beat us to the pit.

Low alarums.

It is more worthy to leap in ourselves,
Than tarry till they push us. Good Volumnius,
Thou knowest that we two went to school together.   30
Even for that our love of old, I prithee,
Hold thou my sword-hilts, whilst I run on it.
VOLUMNIUS: That's not an office for a friend, my lord.

Alarum still.

CLITUS: Fly, fly my lord, there is no tarrying here.
BRUTUS: Farewell to you, and you, and you Volumnius.
Strato, thou hast been all this while asleep.
Farewell to thee too, Strato. Countrymen,
My heart doth joy, that yet in all my life
I found no man, but he was true to me.
I shall have glory by this losing day   40
More than Octavius and Mark Antony
By this vile conquest shall attain unto.
So fare you well at once, for Brutus' tongue
Hath almost ended his life's history.
Night hangs upon mine eyes; my bones would rest,
That have but laboured to attain this hour.

Alarum. Cry within, "Fly, fly, fly!"

CLITUS: Fly my lord, fly!
BRUTUS: Hence! I will follow.

[Exeunt Clitus, Dardanius, and Volumnius.]

I prithee Strato, stay thou by thy lord.
Thou art a fellow of a good respect;   50
Thy life hath had some smatch of honour in it.
Hold then my sword, and turn away thy face,
While I do run upon it. Wilt thou, Strato?

26. *the world* – state of affairs
27. *pit* – There are at least three levels of meaning. *Pit* can refer to the pit of death, to the grave, or to the hole into which hunted animals are driven so that they can be killed.
29. *tarry* – wait too long

Stage Direction: The Alarums continue without interruption.

"There is thus a supreme irony in the last scene of the play, which definitively eliminates the possibility of treating Brutus as a tragic hero, and requires instead that we see the action as a study of political forces. (His prophecy is simple nonsense.)"
– Hugh M. Richmond (b. 1932), professor, University of California, Berkeley

50. *respect* – reputation
51. *smatch* – smack; taste

Act Five • Scene 5

60. *fire* – funeral pyre

65. *entertain* – accept into my service
67. *prefer* – recommend

STRATO: Give me your hand first. Fare you well, my lord.
BRUTUS: Farewell, good Strato.

[Runs on his sword.]

Caesar, now be still:
I killed not thee with half so good a will.

Dies.
Alarum. Retreat. Enter Octavius, Antony, Messala, Lucilius, and the Army.

OCTAVIUS: What man is that?
MESSALA: My master's man. Strato, where is thy master?
STRATO: Free from the bondage you are in, Messala.
The conquerors can but make a fire of him.   60
For Brutus only overcame himself,
And no man else hath honour by his death.
LUCILIUS: So Brutus should be found. I thank thee, Brutus,
That thou hast proved Lucilius' saying true.
OCTAVIUS: All that served Brutus, I will entertain them.
Fellow, wilt thou bestow thy time with me?
STRATO: Ay, if Messala will prefer me to you.
OCTAVIUS: Do so, good Messala.

MESSALA: How died my master, Strato?

STRATO: I held the sword, and he did run on it. 70

MESSALA: Octavius, then take him to follow thee,
That did the latest service to my master.

ANTONY: This was the noblest Roman of them all.
All the conspirators save only he
Did that they did, in envy of great Caesar.
He only, in a general honest thought
And common good to all, made one of them.
His life was gentle, and the elements
So mixed in him, that Nature might stand up
And say to all the world, "This was a man!" 80

OCTAVIUS: According to his virtue, let us use him
With all respect and rites of burial.
Within my tent his bones tonight shall lie,
Most like a soldier ordered honourably.
So call the field to rest, and let's away,
To part the glories of this happy day.

Exeunt omnes.

FINIS.

ᔐ ᔐ ᔐ

74. *save* – except

77. *made one of* – joined
78. *gentle* – noble

81. *use* – treat
84. *ordered* – treated
85. *field* – army
86. *part* – divide

"Can all the Trappings or Equipage of a King or Hero give Brutus half that Pomp and Majesty which he receives from a few lines in Shakespeare?"
– Joseph Addison (1672 – 1719), English poet and essayist

Act Five Considerations

ACT FIVE Scene 1

▶ Review the war of words that occurs before the battle. Is there a clear winner? If so, who? Support your opinion with evidence from the text.

▶ Have your feelings about Cassius changed since the beginning of the play? If so, how and why? Create a collage or write a composition in which you address either (a) how Cassius has changed since Act One, or (b) the character traits of Cassius that have remained constant throughout the play.

ACT FIVE Scenes 2 and 3

▶ Movies can more easily create the effect of large and bloody battle scenes than live theatre. In groups of two or more, discuss how you would stage these two scenes to create the most dramatic impression possible of the battlefield.

▶ This scene contains a number of significant ironies. In groups of two or more, compile a list of three to five statements that deal with the ironies in these scenes. Begin each statement with the following stem: "It is ironic that ..."

ACT FIVE Scene 4

▶ Imagine you are Lucilius. Explain why you impersonated Brutus on the battlefield.

ACT FIVE Scene 5

▶ True tragic heroes go to their deaths free of illusions, usually gaining self-knowledge just before they die. To what extent do you think Brutus fits this criterion?

▶ Strato asks Messala to recommend him to Octavius. Imagine you are Messala and have to put the recommendation in writing. Write a reference letter for Strato.

▶ It was very important for the Elizabethan audience to see at the end of a tragedy that the natural order had been re-established and that domestic peace had been restored. All loose ends had to be dealt with. To what extent does the ending of *Julius Caesar* satisfy these expectations? What do the closing speeches of Antony and Octavius suggest about their characters?

▶ Imagine you are a newspaper or television reporter covering the battle at Philippi. Create a front page of a newspaper or a videotape of a news report of the events leading up to and including the death of Brutus. Be sure to include quotations from, or an interview with, one or more of the combatants.

The 10 Most Challenging Questions about *Julius Caesar*

Shakespeare's works have survived for over 400 years. His plays continue to be read, studied, performed, and enjoyed by people all over the world. Shakespeare's legacy is a host of unforgettable characters in great stories, speaking classic lines that contain some of the most powerful poetry ever written.

Perhaps another important reason why Shakespeare continues to fascinate readers and audiences is that his plays can be interpreted in so many different ways. It is ironic that Shakespeare's greatest strength is perhaps his most frustrating quality.

The play *Julius Caesar* poses a number of very interesting and challenging questions. You are invited to choose one or more of the following for closer focus and study. The end result of your efforts may take the form of a research essay, an independent study project, or a position paper. To address these questions, you will need to probe the text carefully and consult secondary sources. You must also be prepared to take a stand regarding the issues.

1. Whose tragedy is it? Would a better title for the play be *The Tragedy of Marcus Brutus*? Why does Shakespeare name the play after Julius Caesar?

2. Who is the main character in the play: Caesar, Brutus, or Antony? Who, then, is the force in conflict with the main character? Is there anyone in the play who can be considered a villain? If so, who?

3. Act Four, Scene 3, better known as the "quarrel scene," contains two mentions of Portia's death. Opinion is divided among scholars as to whether this was an error on the part of the typesetters in Shakespeare's day or if Brutus, in the second mention, is hoping that the reports he received earlier were wrong. What do you think? Was it an oversight on the part of the editors, or was Brutus hoping for news that contradicted his first report?

4. During the Elizabethan period, it was quite common for stories to be turned into multi-part plays. The story of Henry VI, for example, was told in three parts on the stage. Some scholars believe that *Julius*

Caesar was at one time two separate plays: *Death of Caesar* and *Revenge of Caesar*, and that the editors of the First Folio combined the two into one. What do you think? Explain.

5. Sir Mark Hunter wrote: "There can be no doubt that to Shakespeare's way of thinking, however much he extends sympathy to the perpetrators of the deed, the murder of Julius was the foulest crime in secular history." This interpretation would suggest that during the Elizabethan period the audience's sympathies would have been with Caesar, Antony, and Octavius throughout. The conspirators, except for Brutus, would have been considered traitors and murderers. How do modern audiences interpret the play? Are our sympathies with those loyal to Caesar or with the conspirators who act against tyranny?

6. Does the play take place in Rome or in Shakespeare's England? According to T.J.B. Spencer, "It was apparent that, when it came to details, Shakespeare's Romans often belonged to the time of Queen Elizabeth and King James." Was the play merely a history play dealing with the death of Julius Caesar, or was it much more to the Elizabethan audience? To what extent could it have served as a warning to people about the dangers of overthrowing the ruler of their country? To what extent is this warning valid even today? Explain your ideas fully.

7. Cassius in Act One is not the same as Cassius in the second half of the play. Why would Shakespeare paint a portrait of Cassius as a villain in the first act of the play, only to have him grow in stature by the end of the play?

8. How Stoical is Brutus? What does the philosophy of Stoicism teach? Does Brutus follow this approach to life consistently throughout the play? Explain.

9. Cassius claims to be an Epicurean. What does the philosophy of Epicureanism teach? To what extent does Cassius show himself to be a true Epicurean throughout the play?

10. Shakespeare's source for the play was Thomas North's translation of *Plutarch's Lives*. How faithful was Shakespeare to the source material? What major differences are there between Plutarch's account and Shakespeare's play?

Historical Background

by Isaac Asimov

to JULIUS CAESAR

*How did Caesar become the "foremost man of all this world"? In this
selection, science and science-fiction writer Isaac Asimov provides some
insights into the rise and fall of the mighty Julius Caesar.*

The events of the first scene, in the streets of the city of Rome, are those of October 45 B.C.E. Caesar has just returned from Spain, where he defeated the last armies of those adversaries that had stood out against him.

He was now undisputed master of all the Roman realm, from end to end of the Mediterranean Sea. It seemed Rome was ready now to experience a rich and prosperous period of peace under the great Julius.

Not all of Rome is delighted by this turn of events, however. Those who had opposed Caesar and his policies might have been beaten into silence, but not into approval— and not even always into silence.

Caesar stood for an utter and thoroughgoing reform of the political system of the Roman Republic, which in the last century had fallen into decay and corruption. In this, he was supported chiefly by the commons and opposed chiefly by the senators and the aristocratic families.

In the first scene, though, Shakespeare pictures not the aristocratic opposition, but that of a pair of tribunes, Flavius and Marullus. This is odd, for the office of tribune was originally established to protect the commons against the aristocrats. . . .

One would have thought they would be more likely to support Caesar than oppose him.

Actually, however, the matter of the tribunes is borrowed by Shakespeare from Plutarch, but is moved earlier in time. If the incident had been left in its Plutarchian place, it would have seemed more apt.

At any rate, in Shakespeare's version the populace is swarming out to greet the homecoming Caesar, when they are met by the tribunes. One of them, Flavius, cries out:

*Hence, home you idle creatures, get you
   home!*   (1.1.1)

One of the populace, a cobbler, explains the activity:

*. . . indeed, sir, we make holiday, to see
Caesar and to rejoice in his triumph.*
                                        (1.1.32–33)

The "triumph" was an old Roman custom borrowed from the ancient Etruscans centuries before Caesar's time. A victorious general entered the city in state, preceded by government officials and followed by his army and captured prisoners. The procession moved along decorated streets and between lines of cheering spectators to the Capitol, where religious services were held. (It was rather analogous to the

115

Related Readings

modern ticker-tape procession down Fifth Avenue.)

The day was a high festival, with plenty of food and drink for all at government expense, so that the populace was delighted partly with the aura of victory and partly with the fun. For the general himself, it represented the highest possible honor.

In July 46 B.C.E., more than a year before the play opens, Caesar had returned to Rome after nine years of conquest in Gaul and three years of civil war in Greece, Egypt, Asia Minor, and Africa. He had then broken all public records for magnificence by holding four triumphs, one after another, over each of four sets of foreign enemies he had conquered. These were the Gauls, the Egyptians, the Pontines of Asia Minor, and the Numidians of Africa.

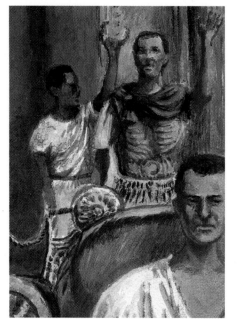

After that, he went to Spain for one last victorious battle, and now he was returning for one last triumph.

The cobbler's reply but further irritates the tribune Marullus, who cries out in anguish:

> *Wherefore rejoice?*
> *What conquest brings he home?*
> *What tributaries follow him to Rome,*
> *To grace in captive bonds his chariot*
> *   wheels?*   (1.1.34–37)

Marullus has a point here. The whole purpose of a triumph was to demonstrate the victories of Romans over their non-Roman enemies—over foreigners. Civil wars in themselves could bring no true conquests; Roman fought Roman so that a Roman victory necessarily implied a Roman defeat as well and a triumph was impossible.

Caesar, in the course of the civil war, had beaten armies under Roman generals, but he had been careful not to celebrate such victories in specific triumphs. He had brought as prisoners only foreigners who had fought against him, even when these (the Numidians, for instance) had been fighting as allies of Roman factions and even though the Roman soldiers who opposed him bore the brunt of the defeat.

In his last battle in Spain, however, there were no foreign enemies. He had fought only Romans and if he had a triumph it could be only over Romans. He did not bring home a true "conquest," no true "tributaries," and why, therefore, a triumph?

The tribunes can be even more specific. Marullus says:

> *Knew you not Pompey? Many a time and*
> *   oft*
> *Have you climbed up to walls and battle-*
> *   ments,*
> *To towers and windows, yea, to*
> *   chimney-tops,*
> *Your infants in your arms, and there have*
> *   sat*
> *The livelong day, with patient expectation,*
> *To see great Pompey pass the streets of*
> *   Rome.*   (1.1.40–45)

Pompey was born in 106 B.C.E. and made a great name for himself as a general at quite an early age, largely because of his talent for being on the right side in the right place at the right time. He won important victories in Spain, for instance, in 77 B.C.E. against a rebellious Roman general, largely because that general happened to be assassinated at the crucial moment.

He was given the right to append "Magnus" ("the Great") to his name as a result of early victories, which accounts for the tribune's reference to "great Pompey."

In 67 B.C.E. he accomplished something really surprising. Pirates had been infesting the Mediterranean Sea for a long time. They had evaded all Roman force and had all but made trade impossible, when Pompey was called to the task of suppressing them. He was put in charge of the entire Mediterranean coast to a distance of fifty miles [80 km] inland for three years and was told to use that time for destroying the pirates. He managed to clear them all out in three months!

He was then put in charge of the Roman armies in Asia Minor. Again, this was a tremendous piece of luck for him. An earlier Roman general, competent but unpopular, had almost completed the job when his troops rebelled. Pompey took over, cleared up the last remaining forces of the enemy, and got all the credit.

In 61 B.C.E. he returned to Rome and at the age of forty-five received the most magnificent triumph Rome had seen up to that time. It is presumably partly with reference to this triumph that the tribunes spoke of the people waiting to see the great Pompey.

Pompey was not of a great aristocratic family himself and would have been proud to be accepted by the senators as one of their own. The senators, however, had learned from experience that successful generals of the non-aristocratic classes could be dangerous, and they watched Pompey carefully.

Yet Pompey had done his best to earn senatorial approval. On returning to Italy in 61 B.C.E. after his victories, he had disbanded

his army and had taken his place in Rome as a private citizen. This had merely gained him a total loss of influence. He could not even persuade the Senate to approve the award of bonuses to his faithful soldiers.

Pompey was forced to turn elsewhere. He formed an alliance with Marcus Licinius Crassus, the richest man in Rome, and with a skillful and charming orator and politician, Julius Caesar. Caesar was then an impoverished aristocrat (who nevertheless opposed the Senators) in the employ of Crassus.

The three together, in 60 B.C.E., formed the First Triumvirate (*triumvir* means "three men") and ruled Rome.

The three took advantage of their power to parcel out provinces for themselves. Caesar, born in 100 B.C.E., and by far the most capable of the three, obtained for himself the governorship of that portion of Gaul ruled by Rome (a portion that included what is now northern Italy and southern France). He used that as a base from which to conquer the rest of Gaul. Fighting his first battles at the age of forty-four, he surprised everyone by showing himself to be a military genius of the first rank.

Pompey, who was assigned the governorship of Spain, but who let deputies run it while he himself remained in Rome, was not entirely pleased by Caesar's sudden development of a military reputation. As for Crassus, he was jealous enough to take an army to the east to fight the Parthians, who ruled over what had once been the eastern part of the Persian Empire. In 53 B.C.E. he lost a catastrophic battle to them at Carrhae,

and lost his life as well.

Pompey and Caesar now shared the power, with no third party to serve as intermediary.

By now the senatorial conservatives, frightened by Caesar's success and recognizing Pompey as far the less dangerous of the two, had lined up solidly behind the latter.

Pompey, flattered by aristocratic attentions, let himself be wooed into open opposition to his erstwhile ally. When Caesar's term as governor of Gaul came to an end, the Senate, buoyed up by Pompey's support, arrogantly ordered Caesar to return to Rome at once without his army. This was technically in order since it was treason for any Roman general to bring a provincial army into Italy.

Caesar, however, knew that if he arrived in Rome without his army, he would be arrested at once on some charge or other, and might well be executed.

So after hesitating at the Rubicon River (the little Italian creek which was the boundary of Italy proper, in the Roman view) he made his decision. On January 10, 49 B.C.E., he crossed the Rubicon with a legion of troops and a civil war began.

Pompey found, much to his own surprise, that Caesar was far more popular than he, and that soldiers flocked to Caesar and not to himself. He was forced to flee to Greece and the senatorial party fled with him. Caesar followed and at a battle in Pharsalia, Greece, on June 29, 48 B.C.E., Caesar's army smashed that of Pompey.

Pompey had to flee again, almost alone,

to Egypt, which was then still independent of Rome. The Egyptian government, however, was afraid to do anything that might displease Caesar, who was clearly the coming man. They therefore assassinated Pompey the instant he landed on Egyptian soil.

Caesar followed, and remained in Egypt for a while. There he met Cleopatra, its fascinating young queen.

Caesar next traveled to Asia Minor, and then to Africa, to defeat die-hard armies allied to those who shared the views of the dead Pompey and the senatorial party. Only then did he return to Rome for his quadruple triumph.

In no part of that quadruple triumph did Caesar commemorate his victory over Pompey himself. In fact, as a deliberate stroke of policy, Caesar forgave such of the Pompeian partisans as he could and did his best to erase hard feelings. His mission, as far as possible, was to unite Rome and put an end to the civil broils through conciliation. . . .

The populace disbands and leaves the stage, presumably returning to their houses in guilt. The tribune, Flavius, then suggests that they tear down the decorations intended for the triumph. Marullus hesitates, for it may be sacrilege. He says:

> *May we do so?*
> *You know it is the Feast of Lupercal.*
> (1.1.69–70)

The Lupercalian festival was an ancient fertility rite whose origins are lost in antiquity and probably predate civilization. It involved the ritual sacrifice of goats, which were noted for being ruttish animals.

Strips of the skin of the sacrificed goats were cut off by the priests in charge. They then ran about the Palatine Hill, striking out with those thongs. Anyone struck would be rendered fertile, supposedly, and sterile women therefore so placed themselves at the rites as to make sure they would be struck.

The "feast of Lupercal" was held each year on February 15 and this was not the day of Caesar's last triumph at all (as would appear from the play), but four months later. Shakespeare, however, commonly compresses time in his historical plays (a compression that is a dramatic necessity, and even a dramatic virtue), and here he lets the four months pass between the driving off of the populace and the next speech of the tribunes. There is no further talk of the triumph. ∎

Outline the major events in Caesar's life that led to his position of power in 45 B.C.E.

According to Asimov, Caesar was much more than a successful general who attained supreme control over the Roman world. What were some of his positive characteristics? What contributions did he make to the Roman state?

Research the military career of Julius Caesar. On a map of the Roman world, shade in the countries that Caesar was directly responsible for conquering.

Related Readings

by C. P. Cavafy

The Ides of March

Caesar's fate serves to warn us of the pitfalls of pride.

Fear grandeurs, O my soul.
And if you cannot triumph over your
ambitions, pursue them with hesitation
and precaution. And the more you go forward,
the more searching, attentive you must be.

And when you reach your peak, Caesar at last;
when you take on the form of a famous man,
then above all take heed as you go out on the street,
a man of authority conspicuous with your followers,
if by chance out of the mob some Artemidorus
should approach you, who brings you a letter,
and hastily says, "Read this at once,
it contains grave matters of concern to you,"
do not fail to stop; do not fail to put off
all talk or work; do not fail to turn away
the various people who salute you and kneel before you
(you can see them later); let even the Senate
itself wait, and immediately get to know
the grave writings of Artemidorus.

What advice does the poem's speaker offer? To whom is the advice addressed?

What other lessons are there to be learned by looking closely at Caesar's fate? Write your own "Ides of March" poem in which you offer advice on how to avoid Caesar's mistakes.

The Fall *of* Rome

by Susan L. Gilbert

"Beware the ides of March!"
Warned the soothsayer—
"On the feast of Lupercal
Beware, beware for your life!"
But Caesar scorned his warning as false dream
And passed him by without thought
Or the unequivocal extent that maybe.
Brutus, his trusted friend, continued by Cassius
Who spoke of Caesar as a colossus
And declared their names as fair.

The sky flamed red like fire
And Cassius proclaimed his stand—
"Caesar will never wear Rome's crown
Neither by sea or land!"
Brutus, meanwhile, Caesar's faithful friend,
Watched the stars in the night sky
And the fate of the mighty Caesar,
As it like a darkening cloud, began to descend.
The conspirators met and conspired
"Caesar shall be served as a God's dish
Bold as he stands,
For his spirit is only one
Against that of many men."

The power of poetry comes from its compactness, its ability to say much in few words. Choose a scene from the play and write a short poem that deals with the events in that scene. Do not hesitate to incorporate quotations from Shakespeare in your poem.

by Sarojini Shintri

CALPURNIA and PORTIA

There are only two female roles in the play Julius Caesar. *According to Shintri, however, Shakespeare has succeeded in painting rich portraits of these two women that emphasize their importance in the tragedy.*

Though their roles are minor, they do not fail to leave [a lasting impression on the reader]. . . . Gentle they are, still not all submissive. They are both women of spirit. Their mainstay in life appears to be the welfare of their husbands. And Caesar and Brutus are worthy of them.

Calpurnia is childless, and Caesar asks her to stand on Mark Antony's course to be touched by him:

CAESAR: Calpurnia!
CALPURNIA: Here my lord.
CAESAR: Stand you directly in Antonio's way
    When he doth run his course. Antonio.
ANTONY: Caesar, my lord?
CAESAR: Forget not, in your speed, Antonio,
    To touch Calpurnia; for our elders say,
    The barren touched in this holy chase,
    Shake off their sterile curse. (1.2.3–11)

She is frightened when she gets bad dreams about Caesar, and entreats him not to stir out that day:

CALPURNIA: O Caesar! These things are beyond all use,
    And I do fear them.
CAESAR: What can be avoided
    Whose end is purposed by the mighty gods?
    Yet Caesar shall go forth, for these predictions
    Are to the world in general as to Caesar.

CALPURNIA: When beggars die, there are no comets seen.
    The heavens themselves blaze forth the death of princes.
CAESAR: Cowards die many times before their deaths;
    The valiant never taste of death but once.
    Of all the wonders that I yet have heard,
    It seems to me most strange that men should fear,
    Seeing that death, a necessary end
    Will come when it will come.   (2.2.26–39)

In spite of it all, however, Caesar gives way to his wife's entreaty. He does not put her off, as he did the soothsayer. There seems to be a happy understanding between the two. It is, indeed, a pity that Shakespeare does not show how she bore the murder of Caesar.

    Portia is more spaciously drawn. The way she persists in knowing the uneasy thoughts of her husband, which made him,

    . . . walk unbraced and suck up the humours
    Of the dank morning   (2.1.274–275)

and

    . . . steal out of his wholesome bed,
    To dare the vile contagion of the night   (2.1.276–277)

is so behoving of a wife who is at once loving but self-respecting. She would like to share the trials and tribulations of her husband. She is his life's partner as much as the mother of his children:

              No, my Brutus.
    You have some sick offence within your mind,
    Which, by the right and virtue of my place,
    I ought to know of. And, upon my knees,
    I charm you, by my once commended beauty,
    By all your vows of love, and that great vow
    Which did incorporate and make us one,
    That you unfold to me, your self, your half,
    Why you are heavy, and what men tonight
    Have had to resort to you;   (2.1.279–288)

She is annoyed that Brutus does not take her into his confidence—

    Is it excepted I should know no secrets
    That appertain to you? Am I your self
    But, as it were in sort or limitation,
    To keep with you at meals, comfort your bed,

And talk to you sometimes? Dwell I but in the suburbs
Of your good pleasure? If it be no more,
Portia is Brutus' harlot, not his wife.   (2.1.294–300)

She takes it as an insult that Brutus will not trust her, as a mere woman, not fit to share the burden of a man's secrets. Had she not shown him how she could bear a wound patiently?

I grant I am a woman, but withal
A woman that Lord Brutus took to wife.
I grant I am a woman, but withal
A woman well reputed, Cato's daughter.
Think you I am no stronger than my sex,
Being so fathered and so husbanded?
Tell me your counsels, I will not disclose 'em.
I have made strong proof of my constancy,
Giving myself a voluntary wound
Here, in the thigh. Can I bear that with patience,
And not my husband's secrets?   (2.1.305–315)

What's the use of his saying to her—

You are my true and honourable wife,
As dear to me as are the ruddy drops
That visit my sad heart.   (2.1.301–303)

Portia is gentle, but she has an individuality, an independence of mind, and a courage to assert her wifely right and her womanly dignity. She has even the courage to question the love of her husband. And it is natural that a man of the calibre of Brutus should love and admire her—

O ye gods,
Render me worthy of this noble wife!   (2.1.316–317)

How do you think Calpurnia bore the murder of Caesar? Write a short scene, either as prose narrative or as dialogue, which deals with Calpurnia's reception of the news that her husband has been assassinated.

What would you add to Shintri's analysis of Portia's character?

I Saw CAESAR Pass in SPLENDOUR

by Richard Woollatt

*This poem attempts to capture the power and
excitement of a live theatrical performance.*

I saw Caesar pass in splendour
at a Stratford playhouse
borne in a chair by four slaves
down the aisle so close
I could have reached up
         clutched his ankle
& sabotaged his triumph . . .
but in that electric moment
I gazed in awe
         like a dumb plebeian
as the laurelled dictator
passed in a cloud of incense

And later, after his
senate-house assassination
when Romans fled up my aisle
shrieking, "Help ho, murder, murder!"
I tensed to join the retreat
         or echo the agonized cry
caught up in that sensuous
         intimate performance
the bard's Roman tragedy
         fleshed out and triumphant.

If you have ever attended a live performance of a Shakespearean play, write a poem
or a paragraph about that experience. If you have not attended such a performance,
write about what you imagine the experience might be like.

by Frank Barone

How to Report on What You've Seen or Read

Watch the way Brutus
an honorable man
deceived by wily Cassius
sticks his knife into
Caesar's ambition
then pick up your pen
and drive the point
deep into the heart
of the play.
Now stand in the Forum
with Mark Antony
and speak
for all the noble Romans
poets and teachers.
Show the slashes
in your toga
your bloody hands
the scars from your battle
with Shakespeare.
Show . . . Truth
not fiction.
I deal in honesty.

What do you think is meant by the last three lines of this poem?

THE KILLING OF JULIUS CAESAR

"LOCALIZED"

*Satirist Mark Twain takes a "stab" at reporting the news
of Caesar's assassination for the* Roman Daily Evening Fasces.

NOTHING IN THE WORLD AFFORDS A NEWSPAPER REPORTER SO MUCH SATISFACTION AS GATHERING UP THE DETAILS OF A BLOODY AND MYSTERIOUS MURDER, AND WRITING THEM UP WITH AGGRAVATING CIRCUMSTANTIALITY. HE TAKES A LIVING DELIGHT IN THIS LABOR OF LOVE—FOR SUCH IT IS TO HIM, ESPECIALLY IF HE KNOWS THAT ALL THE OTHER PAPERS HAVE GONE TO PRESS, AND HIS WILL BE THE ONLY ONE THAT WILL CONTAIN THE DREADFUL INTELLIGENCE. A FEELING OF REGRET HAS OFTEN COME OVER ME THAT I WAS NOT REPORTING IN ROME WHEN CAESAR WAS KILLED. . . .

HOWEVER, AS I WAS NOT PERMITTED TO REPORT CAESAR'S ASSASSINATION IN THE REGULAR WAY, IT HAS AT LEAST AFFORDED ME RARE SATISFACTION TO TRANSLATE THE FOLLOWING ABLE ACCOUNT OF IT FROM THE ORIGINAL LATIN OF THE *ROMAN DAILY EVENING FASCES* OF THAT DATE—SECOND EDITION.

"Our usually quiet city of Rome was thrown into a state of wild excitement yesterday by the occurrence of one of those bloody affrays which sicken the heart and fill the soul with fear, while they inspire all thinking men with forebodings for the future of a city where human life is held so cheaply, and the gravest laws are so openly set at defiance. As the result of that affray, it is our painful duty, as public journalists, to record the death of one of our most esteemed citizens . . . Mr. J. Caesar, the Emporer-elect.

"The facts of the case, as nearly as our reporter could determine them from the conflicting statements of eye-witnesses, were about as follows:—The affair was an election row, of course. . . . It is said that when the immense majority for Caesar at the polls in the market was declared the other day, and the crown was offered to that gentleman, even his amazing unselfishness in refusing it three times was not sufficient to save him from the whispered insults of such men as Casca . . . and other hirelings of the disappointed candidate, . . . who were overheard speaking ironically and contemptuously of Mr. Caesar's conduct upon that occasion. . . .

"The Senate was already in session, and Caesar was coming down the street towards the Capitol, conversing with some personal friends, and followed, as usual, by a large number of citizens. Just as he was passing in front of Demosthenes and Thucydides' drugstore, he was observing casually to a gentleman, who, our informant thinks, is a fortune-teller, that the Ides of March were come. The reply was, 'Yes, they are come, but not gone yet.' At this moment Artemidorus stepped up and passed the time of day, and asked Caesar to read a schedule or a tract or something of the kind, which he had brought for his perusal. Mr. Decius Brutus also said something about an 'humble suit' which *he* wanted read. Artemidorus begged that attention might be paid to his first, because it was of personal consequence to Caesar. The latter replied that what concerned himself should be read last, or words to that effect. Artemidorus begged and beseeched him to read the paper instantly. However, Caesar shook him off, and refused to read any petition in the street. He then entered the Capitol, and the crowd followed him.

"About this time the following conversation was overheard, and we consider that, taken in connection with the events which succeeded it, it bears an appalling significance: Mr. Papilius Lena remarked to George W. Cassius . . . , a bruiser in the pay of the Opposition, that he hoped his enterprise today might thrive; and when Cassius asked 'What enterprise?' he only closed his left eye temporarily and said with simulated indifference, 'Fare you well,' and sauntered towards Caesar. Marcus Brutus, who is suspected of being the ringleader of the band that killed Caesar, asked what it was that Lena had said. Cassius told him, and added in a low tone, '*I fear our purpose is discovered.*'

"Brutus told his wretched accomplice to keep an eye on Lena, and a moment after Cassius urged that lean and hungry vagrant, Casca, whose reputation here is none of the best, to be sudden for *he feared prevention.* He then turned to Brutus, apparently much excited, and asked what should be done, and swore that either he or Caesar *should*

never turn back—he would kill himself first. At this time Caesar was talking to some of the back-country members about the approaching fall elections, and paying little attention to what was going on around him. Billy Trebonius got into conversation with the people's friend and Caesar's—Mark Antony—and under some pretence or other got him away, and Brutus, Decius, Casca, Cinna, Metellus Cimber, and others of the gang of infamous desperadoes that infest Rome at present, closed around the doomed Caesar. Then Metellus Cimber knelt down and begged that his brother might be recalled from banishment, but Caesar rebuked him for his fawning conduct, and refused to grant his petition. Immediately, at Cimber's request, first Brutus and then Cassius begged for the return of the banished Publius; but Caesar still refused. He said he could not be moved; that he was as fixed as the North Star, and proceeded to speak in the most complimentary terms of the firmness of that star and its steady character. Then he said he was like it, and he believed he was the only man in the country that was; therefore, since he was 'constant' that Cimber should be banished, he was also 'constant' that he should stay banished, and he'd be hanged if he didn't keep him so!

"Instantly seizing upon this shallow pretext for a fight, Casca sprang at Caesar and struck him with a dirk, Caesar grabbing him by the arm with his right hand, and launching a blow straight from the shoulder with his left, that sent the reptile bleeding to the earth. He then backed up against Pompey's statue, and squared himself to receive his assailants. Cassius and Cimber and Cinna rushed upon him with their daggers drawn, and the former succeeded in inflicting a wound upon his body; but before he could strike again, and before either of the others could strike at all, Caesar stretched the three miscreants at his

feet with as many blows of his powerful fist. By this time the Senate was in an indescribable uproar; the throng of citizens in the lobbies had blockaded the doors in their frantic efforts to escape from the building, the sergeant-at-arms and his assistants were struggling with the assassins, venerable senators had cast aside their encumbering robes, and were leaping over benches and flying down the aisles in wild confusion towards the shelter of the committee-rooms, and a thousand voices were shouting 'Po-lice! Po-lice!' in discordant tones that rose above the frightful din like shrieking winds above the roaring of a tempest. And amid it all, great Caesar stood with his back against the statue, like a lion at bay, and fought his assailants weaponless and hand to hand, with the defiant bearing and the unwavering courage which he had shown before on many a bloody field. Billy Trebonius and Caius Legarius struck him with their daggers and fell, as their brother-conspirators before them had fallen. But at last, when Caesar saw his old friend Brutus step forward armed with a murderous knife, it is said he seemed utterly overpowered with grief and amazement, and dropping his invincible left arm by his side, he hid his face in the folds of his mantle and received the treacherous blow without an effort to stay the hand that gave it. He only said '*Et tu, Brute?*' and fell lifeless on the marble pavement." ■

Imagine that you work for the same newspaper as Twain's fictional reporter. Write a companion item that would have appeared along with this front page news story. It can be a related news article, column, editorial, review, obituary, sports story, or any other feature commonly found in newspapers.

Related Readings

by G.W.F. Hegel

translated from German
by Christiane Seiler

A CONVERSATION
of Three

▲　▲　▲

*German philosopher Hegel, at the age of fifteen and while still a
student, wrote this adaptation of Act Four, Scene 1 of* Julius
Caesar. *But Hegel does more than adapt Shakespeare—he adds
insight into the character of Octavius.*

ANTONIUS: Have you both thought over the plan I presented to
you? Any conclusions yet?

OCTAVIUS: I have given it consideration and indeed much thought.
If it is carried out as happily as is suggested by its wise and
intelligent arrangement, something quite magnificent will come
of it.

LEPIDUS: It impressed me the same way.

OCTAVIUS: Yes, but how? We must identify particulars of the
matter and the obstacles ahead.

ANTONIUS: After due thought, I have not found any special
difficulties.

OCTAVIUS: But I have. Let me lay them out. Will the free Romans
immediately agree to our rule? Brutus, Cassius, and the others
who helped kill the noble Caesar, will they silently assent? Will
we be able to satisfy Sextus Pompeius?

ANTONIUS: Have no such scruples, my good Octavius! Believe me,
I have lived longer in this world and have more experience than
you. Do you believe that in these Romans there still glows even
a spark of patriotism? Not in the least! Through luxury and
debauchery they have lost so much of their ancestral greatness
of soul that liberty no longer means anything to them. Soon
after Caesar's murder, when Brutus and Cassius stood on the
tribune and had inflamed such hatred against the great Julius
that, out of madness, they would almost have profaned his
sacred corpse, how much eloquence did I need to change their
tone? They allow themselves to be blown to and fro like
feathers. The soldier is used to shedding the blood of citizens as
much as that of the enemy. And the soldier we have safely on
our side. For the vulgar mob a few words are sufficient. Some
corn or money and public spectacles will do.

LEPIDUS: I will see to this.

OCTAVIUS: You're perfectly right, Antonius. *One* concern is now eliminated. Yet a Brutus or a Cassius is far above the sphere of the mob.

ANTONIUS: But these two, my Octavius, have lost all public significance, all love and respect through Caesar's murder and my speech. The people are safely on our side. What can they possibly do? So far we've not heard a thing from them.

OCTAVIUS: Yet it's scarcely been four hours since I received letters indicating their most secret mobilization for defense. They fear us. I was going to tell you of the news at once, but you were neither at the Capitol nor at home.

ANTONIUS: I was staying at my country-seat. But the fact that Brutus and Cassius are preparing war causes me no such great concern. We are warriors as well as they. We merely have to be on our guard, unite our forces, and thus convene at once our legates and tribunes.

131

OCTAVIUS: But quite apart from these there are still many foes who, to be sure, show friendliness on their face, and yet conceal poisonous daggers in their hearts. They must be removed.

ANTONIUS: So they must, my Octavius. We have discussed all this in our last meeting, have designated most of them by name, and vowed their death. I have them recorded here. Read it through!

OCTAVIUS: *[Reads and suddenly exclaims.]* Even Cicero?

ANTONIUS: Quite so, Octavius. At our last meeting we decided to leave it up to each to dispatch into the kingdom of the dead whomever he may have chosen. Cicero was my deadly enemy. His speeches and letters prove it only too well. Has not Lepidus ceded even his brother to you?

LEPIDUS: True, so have I done.

OCTAVIUS: My word once given can never be withdrawn, but I feel in very great pain over the man.

ANTONIUS: Here, Lepidus, why don't you read this, too. At your behest even my uncle Lucius stands among the condemned. So it all evens out between us. Each has sacrificed to our common welfare a man who causes him pain. But let's turn now to another matter, the parceling out of lands.

OCTAVIUS: This is a matter, I think, we'd rather let lie for now. We don't want to resolve that until after subduing Brutus and Cassius. Yet we have seriously to consider counter-measures against these enemies.

ANTONIUS: I thought you and I could leave Rome, muster our army and attack them in their provinces. Lepidus can hold the city. What do you say?

OCTAVIUS: Fine, perfect.

LEPIDUS: I am agreed. But I had best be off now to take the necessary steps.

[Lepidus exits.]

ANTONIUS: So now you are off, you fatuous man! I want to talk openly with you alone, Octavius. Should we let this barren head take part someday in the domination of the world?

OCTAVIUS: But it was you who dragged him into this union. Matters can probably now never be undone. Yet I think in many places he has proven a brave soldier.

ANTONIUS: Mark my word, I have come to know the man. He has no inherent merit, no mental capacities. He has ability only for the skillful execution of missions. Like a lifeless machine he has to be set in motion by others. Believe me, if he didn't have powerful friends it would have never entered my mind to take him in. For the present we need him. But once we reach our mark in life, once we find ourselves sufficiently strong, I say we should no longer wait to relieve him of his undeserved post of honor — we should fatten him with stubble or get rid of him altogether. We shall then feast on the ears which he has so thoughtfully planted and harvested for us.

OCTAVIUS: I leave it to your judgment. We can discuss the matter further after a favorable unfolding of our plans. — But right now, Antonius, we must take heed. Closer and more violent storms are gathering over our head. We want to ready our forces without delay, so as to courageously defy the raging storm soon to descend.

ANTONIUS: Yes, quite right. But before we leave I have to straighten out a few things. Perhaps we'll talk again tonight. Till then farewell!

[Antonius exits.]

OCTAVIUS: *[Alone.]* No sooner does idiocy exit than wantonness follows right behind! What Antonius says about Lepidus is completely true. Antonius, however, is proud, imperious, voluptuous, and cruel. When our enemies are defeated and Lepidus removed, Antonius, proud of his deeds and experience, will lead me as the younger man around at will. Yet in me he will find no Lepidus! My unslavish neck is not accustomed to bend under the defamatory glances of a ruler! He will toss about in voluptuousness. I will quietly tolerate it for a long time. Only when his physical and mental faculties have slackened and he encounters disdain, will I want to raise my head and unveil to him my true dimensions. *Aut Caesar, aut nihil!* Either he will humble himself before me in the dust, or I shall prefer death to life without honor.

[Exit.]

ह ह ह

How does Hegel's version of the scene compare with the original? Outline the similarities and differences. Which do you prefer? Why?

Hegel develops Octavius' character in the concluding soliloquy. Using this strategy, develop some aspects of Antony's character by writing a concluding soliloquy for him. Be sure that what you write is consistent with what we know of Antony in the play.

Related Readings

by Phyllis Bentley

Freedom, Farewell!

Bentley's tale takes place shortly after Caesar's assassination. It is a matter of historical record that after Caesar's murder, Antony's foremost adversary was the orator Cicero. This story sheds light on why Antony insists that Cicero's name be "pricked" for death.

The pleas of Brutus that he should return to Rome were exactly what Cicero wished to hear; to be told his presence was necessary to the safety of the Republic was highly agreeable to the old orator, who still looked back wistfully to the great days of his consulship. When Antony summoned the Senate for the first day of September, Cicero therefore decided to attend, and returned to Rome for the purpose. But on his arrival he learned that the business of the day was the decree of some further extraordinary honours to the dead Caesar, and actually to order supplications to him as a divinity. A temple was indeed to be erected to him, and dedicated to the Divine Julius and his Fortune.

"The divine Julius!" exclaimed Cicero, opening his large childlike eyes wide in horror. "A baldhead among the gods! What impiety!"

This remark, being repeated with gusto all over Rome, reached the ears of Antony, who therefore had strong reason to suspect that Cicero's excuse of fatigue for his absence on the day of the decree was false, as indeed it was. Furious, Antony spoke angrily against Cicero, threatening him with all kinds of punishments for non-attendance.

On the following day, Cicero therefore went to the Senate, and when asked his opinion on some of the business before the house, took the opportunity to defend himself. He began his speech mildly, with an account of his motives for leaving Rome and for returning, and actually praised Antony for his judicious behaviour at the time of Caesar's death. In truth he was nervous, not only with his customary nervousness when beginning an oration, but also because it was months since he had spoken in public, and he felt unsure of himself and his powers. But as he proceeded, and the Senate listened attentively, he gathered courage. It was so delightful to be speaking again! To see that look of rapt attention, to watch men's faces change at his words! O, it was glorious!

"As for this shocking act, this inexplicable impiety of joining a dead man with a religious observance," cried Cicero in his beautiful sonorous tones: "I pray only that the immortal gods may pardon it, and not impute it as a crime to Rome."

A thrill ran through the Senate, and thence through Cicero's heart. Now he held them in the hollow of his hand, to wake or soothe, to melt or fire, at his will! He forgot everything but his grievance and his eloquence; bright burning sentences accusing Antony flowed like lava from his lips; he laughed at Antony, and the Senate could not but laugh; he raged at him, and the Senate could not but rage. The oration had a magnificent success. At its close Cicero felt himself back in his old place of influence and power. His large eyes beamed, his thinning blood ran fast again; he was happy, eager, busy, Cicero the father of his country once more!

The infuriated Antony had an answering oration composed for him, learned it word for word and practised it for fourteen days before venturing to deliver it in the Senate. Cicero, naturally following the lines of his previous success, in reply composed a speech so bitter, so vehement, that it could not safely be delivered; it was copied out, however, and passed about the City, sent to Brutus and Cassius, who had now left Italy to take up their provinces, read all over the Roman world.

And for the next six months Cicero continued to pour out these impassioned denunciations vigorously and joyously, and in order further to vex Antony, sustained the pretensions of Octavius in every possible way. Antony changed the allotment of the provinces in favour of his own partisans, and took up arms ostensibly to enforce the change; Octavius, who as Caesar's adopted son had influence with Caesar's dreaded veterans, was encouraged by the Senate, under Cicero's influence, to arm and oppose him. Antony at this point complained with justice that two Caesarian armies were fighting each other like gladiators, with Cicero for a trainer; at this Cicero chuckled with glee, attacked Antony more and more fiercely, fawned upon Octavius more and more tenderly. He saw himself as the arbiter of the fortunes of the Republic, holding the scale between these two legatees of Caesar—when Octavius rose, Antony necessarily sank, he thought; presently Antony would fall altogether to the ground, then the scale holding Octavius would fly up and dislodge him too. Meanwhile, Cicero held the balance, Cicero the orator, the father of the State! Delightful! Brutus from abroad wrote in alarm to him repeatedly, reproving his slavish treatment of Octavius, begging for caution. "If you will only see the depth of my alarm in regard to him!" besought Brutus. But Cicero pursued his own policy of playing off one enemy of the Republic against another cheerfully—

infuriating Antony and behaving as gently to Octavius, as he said, as an ear-lap—sure that it was the right one. Lepidus, the Pontifex Maximus, suddenly went over to Antony with a few legions; it was awkward, but Cicero felt no real alarm, for Antony had Octavius against him—and when Antony was finished, the Republic would finish Octavius. The young Caesar, as Cicero neatly put it, was in every way to be complimented, honoured, and sent aloft.

This ambiguous remark was repeated to Octavius, who observed in his suave flat tones that he did not mean to soar in any sense except the honourable one. A calculating look appeared on his face as he spoke, and presently he smiled thoughtfully; he had now received everything he needed—rank, money, legions—from the Senate, and could afford to discard it and proceed to his real designs.

The raft, poled by an old ferryman, moved slowly across the dull sluggish waters towards the island. It was November, and a chilly mist hung over this river of Northern Italy. Octavius, who viewed rivers, rafts, and mists with an equally intense dislike, shivered and pulled his toga more closely about him. He quite agreed, however, that an island in the middle of a river, where armies were necessarily out of call on the banks, was the only safe place for a meeting between Antony, himself, and Lepidus; he certainly would not trust himself in Antony's camp till they had agreed on terms, and did not blame Antony for feeling the same about his own. Lepidus was really negligible, but useful as representing religion, and to make a third in the alliance; Octavius had not forgotten that Pompey and the divine Julius did not quarrel until after Crassus was dead. Attended only by his secretary, therefore, Octavius was making this disagreeable journey on this chilly day, to arrange for the conduct of the Roman government by these three men.

Related Readings

Antony and Lepidus had already reached the island, and stood on the soaking grass before the tent watching his approach; they evidently did not wish to do him either the honour of advancing to meet him, or the affront of receiving him as a mere guest in the tent. Octavius avoided this little difficulty by affecting not to see them at all; he minced up the roughly trodden path with his eyes down and a preoccupied expression. The tent was warmed, he was pleased to observe, by a charcoal brazier; a marble pavement had been laid, and draped chairs set about a table with writing materials. He observed that Antony and Lepidus both wore military dress, and for a moment regretted his own toga; but he was not fond of military garb, which exposed the thinness of his shanks deplorably, and to wear a different dress from theirs after all distinguished him—he contrived skilfully to seat himself between them, as though presiding. Lepidus began a formal greeting, but Antony cut him short.

"We needn't waste time with formalities," he said in a loud tone of disgust. "We've wasted too much already, fighting each other like two gladiators with Cicero as a trainer." He was proud of this comparison, which he repeated on every possible occasion, and went on now in a better humour: "Our interests are the same."

"Just so—we wish to avenge my father's murder," drawled Octavius.

Antony, who hated to think of this thin pale lad with his silly weak voice as Caesar's son, and was maddened by the suggestion that anyone had been nearer to Caesar than he, scowled and made no reply, and Octavius took the opportunity to slip in what was for him the essential point in the negotiation:

"Our position can be confirmed later by law—a good title would be: triumvirs for counselling the Republic."

Antony stared at him. He was not much given to abstract considerations, but he did spare a moment now to wondering how this insignificant lad had managed to worm himself into a position on a level with Marcus Antonius, consul, master of the horse to Caesar. He knew the answer, however; it was simply Cicero. Antony made a convulsive movement of his hands, then, since facts were facts and the power of Octavius could not be denied, controlled himself and said thickly:

"The title doesn't matter a snap of the fingers to me. What matters is the steps we take to secure ourselves and avenge Caesar."

Octavius, with a slight sigh of relief for Antony's admission of his equal right in the triumvirate, said briskly:

"There will be a proscription, I suppose."

"Yes, by Hercules!" shouted Antony. "A proscription and a long one!"

Octavius gazed at him distastefully. His new ally's physical appearance—the enormous muscles of his heavy shoulders, his brown hairy arms with the barbaric gold bracelets, his thickly curling hair, fiery eyes, and bronzed face—were as repulsive to him as Antony's thirst for blood.

"The murderers will head the list, of course," he said in the sweetly righteous tone he always used when speaking of the tyrannicides.

"Brutus and Cassius first," agreed Lepidus, making a note of the names on his tablets.

"You can put them down, yes," said Antony impatiently. "But we shall have to *fight* them, in their provinces. The proscription is for enemies in Rome."

"Have you any one especially in mind?" drawled Octavius, watching him from beneath half-closed lids.

"Yes! Cicero!" thundered Antony.

Lepidus wrote down *M.T. Cicero*, murmuring: "His son too, I suppose?"

But a slight frown appeared on Octavius' girlish brow.

"It will look bad," he demurred. "It will look very bad. And what harm has Cicero done us, after all?"

"A very popular figure," agreed Lepidus, erasing the entry with the flat end of his stilus, "and harmless."

"Harmless!" shouted Antony, his face purpling. "Harmless!" He struck the table with his fist so that his bracelets jingled and the pens danced. "If the proscription lacks Cicero, your triumvirate lacks me!" he bellowed.

Octavius sighed. "Very well," he agreed mildly, sniffing. "Cicero."

Cicero lay on a bed in his villa near Formiae, face downward, his head covered. When the first list of those proscribed by the triumvirate reached Rome, and he discovered his own name amongst the three hundred, he fled to the coast and took ship, meaning to leave Italy. But it was winter, the sea was rough, and he was old; he could not bear the thought of exile, could not believe that Octavius would so betray him; he landed again in the south and journeyed ten or twelve miles back towards Rome. But all he met expressed such horror at seeing him, such alarm that he was still in Italy, within Antony's reach, that he took fright again, turned aside to this villa on the coast, and commanded his slaves again to find him a ship. Hardly had his steward left him on this errand, however, than he was called back, and returned to find Cicero sitting up on the bed, shouting wildly.

"No, no!" cried the old orator, his eyes dilated. "I will not leave Italy. I will return to Rome. Octavius will not dare to hurt me—the young Caesar, I mean; I have always called him Caesar. I am the father of my country. My consulship was the most glorious in the history of Rome. I saved the Republic!"

His slaves exchanged sad glances; alas, the Republic today was very far from being saved. Cicero, staring from one to another eagerly, read their thoughts. His face quivered; tears filled his old eyes and began to course slowly down his wrinkled cheeks.

"I will go and kill myself on Caesar's hearth," he murmured pitifully, "and so bring a curse on him. Get my litter, you." Since no one stirred, he screamed out angrily: "My litter! Quick! Quick! I go to Rome!"

"It will be wiser not, sir," hesitated a slave.

Cicero, restored for the moment to his senses, groaned and threw himself back on his pillows. The slaves stood there wretchedly, watching him, not knowing what to do for the best.

"Leave me," murmured Cicero at length. "I must think—I must consider."

The slaves withdrew in some relief, but stood about his door whispering, their hearts full of pity for their master. The villa was unprovisioned, since Cicero's arrival had been unexpected, and they had sent a young slave out for food and wine. The lad now came rushing back in a panic; panting and fearful, he gasped out that there were soldiers on the road above.

"What!" exclaimed the steward, horrorstruck.

"There's a centurion and fifty soldiers, and another officer of higher rank," panted the boy. "I think he's a military tribune. They're asking for the villa of Cicero—they're coming this way."

There was a stir of alarm and horror among the slaves.

"We can't let him stay here," said the steward impatiently. "Whatever he says, we must get him to the sea. Bring in his litter."

He threw open the doors of Cicero's room and marched in firmly. "Here is your litter, sir," he announced in a loud clear tone, as if to a child or a fool. "We are taking you to the shore."

Cicero gazed up at him piteously. "I don't want to go," he said in a sad confused mumble. "I don't know where to go. I must think—I must consider."

"You can do that in the litter, sir," urged the steward, listening in a sweat of fear for the sound of soldiers marching. "When you are on the ship,

you can decide then whether to seek Marcus Brutus in Macedonia, or return to Rome."

"True, true," murmured Cicero, nodding his massive old head. "I can decide on board."

The steward suddenly thought he heard a trumpet. "Quick, quick, sir!" he cried in a panic. He seized Cicero under the arms and raised him; another slave took his feet; between them they bundled the protesting old man into the litter, and soon hurried it out of the house and down one of the shady lanes sloping to the sea.

It was close upon sunset; the line of mountains curving round the bay to the northwest was very clear and dark against the golden sky; in the paler east a soft pink cloud hung motionless. Everything was still, cool, calm; not a breath of wind stirred the gnarled branches. It seemed impossible that such a peaceful evening could be desecrated by violence; the steward and the slaves, Cicero himself, began to recover from their first panic, and when at a turn in the lane they caught a glimpse of the smooth unruffled evening sea, they quite took heart and allowed themselves to feel less anxious. Just at this moment, however, a noise arose behind them; the sound of blows on wood, shouts, commands.

"They are at the villa!" whispered the steward, his large face ashen. "Hurry!"

The litter-bearers, gasping and sweating with fear and haste, quickened their step. But it was useless; after a silence, running footsteps and shouts suddenly sounded to their right.

"Turn aside here!" whispered the steward frantically.

The bearers swung off into the olive grove; the litter jarred from side to side as they hurried down the rough path. But this too was useless; in a moment they heard steps ahead of them, and even glimpsed the red and bronze of soldiers, through the trees.

"Turn this way!" whispered the steward, almost weeping.

"No!" cried Cicero suddenly. He drew aside the litter curtains, and commanded, in a tone trembling but determined: "Set me down here. Flight is useless. I cannot escape."

The bearers, perplexed, halted, and at the same moment the soldiers caught sight of them. With savage cries of joy they rushed upon the litter; the bearers, seeing resistance to be useless, set it down and stood back. Cicero leaned out, and called for the tribune. From the exigencies of his flight he was unshaven, and his hair and clothes were tumbled and soiled; nevertheless his face, worn by his troubles, had an air of dignity as, fumbling for his chin with his left hand in the familiar gesture he had used a thousand times in the Senate, he said in a tired sad tone:

"Come! Finish it quickly."

The tribune made a sign. Cicero's slaves gasped and covered their faces as the centurion drew his sword and with two strong blows struck off their master's head.

He then proceeded to sever the orator's hands.

"What are you doing?" cried the steward, weeping. "Do not insult him—he was noble and learned, and a lover of Rome."

"Antony's orders," explained the centurion calmly. "The hands that wrote Cicero's speeches, and the tongue that delivered them. That's so, isn't it, sir?" he added, turning to the tribune.

"That is so—you have done your duty," agreed the tribune, looking a little pale. ◼

How does the death of those such as Cicero mark the end of freedom for Romans?

Cicero's death was a noteworthy event. Write an editorial or obituary celebrating Cicero's life and accomplishments. Include a quotation from this story that would serve as a title for the editorial or a fitting epitaph for his tombstone.

Write Antony's funeral oration for Cicero. Begin with Antony stating that he comes "to bury Cicero and not to praise him."

Related Readings

by Dana K. Haight

The Bitterness of Love

Portia is one of Shakespeare's most intriguing female characters. In this poem,
Haight attempts to plumb the depths of Portia's complexity.

Daughter to Cato,

wife to Lord Brutus,

I imagine you poised

holding perhaps a knife, glistening

freshly sharpened

close to your thigh

ready to slice the peachlike flesh

as a doctor might prepare to remove a tumor.

But your tumor is love,

your intent not to excise

but to tap and spill

to let the red drops bead and ooze along the cut

until they stream a path around the curve of
    your leg

and fall to water the dark earth.

I wonder if you shivered

at the coldness of the blade,

the liquidity of your devotion.

Another woman might have pressed quickly

the knife into the skin,

looking away all the while.

I imagine you,

singly atoning for your father's grief

your husband's melancholy

slow and deliberate

as you apply pressure to the edge,

watching carefully,

pressing the skin together

to force

the blood inherited from your father,

offered for your lord.

When I tremble with the bitterness of love,

I think of Portia,

who swallowed fire to consume the scar
    on her thigh

and everything else she had loved.

According to this poem, why did Portia stab herself in the thigh and why did she "swallow fire"?

Write a short poem either about Portia or dedicated to her.

Bugbears by

MOONLIGHT

by H. N. Hudson

*Hudson argues that many of the perplexing problems of the play
disappear when one appreciates that Shakespeare presents Caesar
not as he truly was but rather as the conspirators saw him.*

It has been justly observed that Shakespeare shows much judgment in the naming of his plays. From this observation, however, several critics have excepted [*Julius Caesar*], pronouncing the title a misnomer, on the ground that Brutus, and not Caesar, is the hero of it. It is indeed true that Brutus is the hero; nevertheless . . . the play is rightly named, inasmuch as Caesar is not only the subject but also the governing power of it throughout. He is the centre and springhead of the entire action, giving law and shape to everything that is said and done. This is manifestly true in what occurs before his death; and it is true in a still deeper sense afterwards, since his genius then becomes the Nemesis . . . presiding over the whole course of the drama.

The characterization of this drama in some of the parts is not a little perplexing to me. . . . For instance, Caesar is far from being himself in these scenes; hardly one of the speeches put into his mouth can be regarded as historically characteristic; taken all together, they are little short of a down-right caricature. As here represented, he is indeed little better than a grand, strutting

piece of puff-paste; and when he speaks, it is very much in the style of a . . . braggart, full of lofty airs and mock-thunder; . . . nothing could be further from the truth of the man, whose character, even in his faults, was as compact and solid as adamant, and at the same time as limber and ductile as the finest gold.

It is true, Caesar's ambition was indeed gigantic, but none too much so, I suspect, for the mind it dwelt in; for his character in all its features was gigantic.

Yet we have ample proof that Shakespeare understood Caesar thoroughly; and that he regarded him as "the noblest man that ever lived in the tide of times."

Indeed, it is clear from this play itself that the Poet's course did not proceed at all from ignorance or misconception of the man. For it is remarkable that, though Caesar delivers himself so out of character, yet others, both foes and friends, deliver him much nearer the truth; so that, while we see almost nothing of him directly, we nevertheless get, upon the whole, a pretty just reflection of him. Especially, in the marvellous speeches of Antony and in the later events of the drama, both his inward greatness and his right of mastership over the Roman world are fully vindicated. For, in the play as in the history, Caesar's blood just hastens and cements the empire which the conspirators thought to prevent. . . . He proves indeed far mightier in death than in life.

And so it was in fact. For nothing did so much to set the people in love with royalty, both name and thing, as the reflection that their beloved Caesar, the greatest of their national heroes, the crown and consummation of Roman genius and character, had been murdered for aspiring to it. Thus their hereditary aversion to kingship was all subdued by the remembrance of how and why their Caesar fell; and they who, before, would have plucked out his heart rather than he should wear a crown, would now have plucked out their own, to set a crown upon his head. Such is the natural result when the intensities of admiration and compassion meet together in the human breast.

From which it may well be thought that Caesar was too great for the hero of a drama, since his greatness, if brought forward in full measure, would leave no room for anything else. . . . At all events, it is pretty clear that, where he was, such figures as Brutus and Cassius could never be very considerable, save as his assassins. They would not have been heard of in aftertimes, if they had not "struck the foremost man of all this world" (4.3.23); in other words, the great sun of Rome had to be shorn of his beams, else so ineffectual a fire as Brutus could nowise catch the eye.

Be this as it may, I have no doubt that Shakespeare knew the whole height and compass of Caesar's vast and varied capacity. And I sometimes regret that he did not render him as he evidently saw him, inasmuch as he alone perhaps of all . . . who ever wrote could have given an adequate expression of that colossal man.

I have sometimes thought that the policy of the drama may have been to represent Caesar, not as he was indeed, but as he must have appeared to the conspirators; to make us see him as they saw him; in order that they too might have fair and equal judgment at our hands. For Caesar was literally too great to be seen by them, save as children often see bugbears by moonlight, when their inexperienced eyes are mocked with air. ■

Hudson suggests that Caesar was perceived by the conspirators in the same way as children "often see bugbears by moonlight." What does this remark mean? Compile a series of arguments that support this opinion. Then do the same with arguments that challenge it. Which position do you agree with?

Dream and Interpretation: JULIUS CAESAR

by Marjorie B. Garber

According to Garber, dreams and their interpretations play an important part in the development of the tragedy in this play.

In the final act of *Julius Caesar*, Cassius, fearful of defeat at Philippi, dispatches Titinius to discover whether the surrounding troops are friends or enemies. He posts another soldier to observe, and when the soldier sees Titinius encircled by horsemen and reports that he is taken, Cassius runs on his sword and dies. Shortly afterward, Titinius reenters the scene bearing a "wreath of victory" from Brutus. When he sees the dead body, he at once understands Cassius' tragic mistake. "Alas, thou hast misconstrued everything" (5.3.90), he cries out, and he too runs on Cassius' sword.

That one cry, "thou hast misconstrued everything," might well serve as an epigraph for the whole of *Julius Caesar*. The play is full of omens and portents, augury and dream, and almost without exception these omens are misinterpreted. Calpurnia's dream, the dream of Cinna the poet, the advice of the augurers, all suggest one course of action and produce its opposite. . . .

Much of the plot of *Julius Caesar* . . . is shaped by the device of the predictive dream or sign. . . . The motif of the misinterpreted dream in this play becomes a main factor in the dramatic action, demonstrating, always, some crucial fact about the interpreter. In the second scene of the play the soothsayer's warning goes unheeded, though in the same scene Caesar betrays his superstitious cast of mind. The contrast is adeptly managed: Antony is reminded to touch Calpurnia in the course of his race on the Lupercal, to remove her "sterile curse" (1.2.11). But when the soothsayer cautions Caesar to "beware the ides of March" (1.2.21), he rejects the intended warning out of hand: "He is a dreamer, let us leave him. Pass" (1.2.28). The inference is that dreams, like omens, are of no value; "dreamer" is a perjorative dismissal, akin to "madman". . . .

Calpurnia's dream is one of the play's cruxes. By this time in the course of the drama an internal convention has been established regarding dreams and omens: whatever their source, they are true, and it is dangerous to disregard them. Shakespeare's audience would certainly have been familiar with the story of Julius Caesar, and such a collection of portents and premonitions would have seemed to them, as it does to us, to be infallibly leading to the moment of murder. Calpurnia herself adds to the catalogue of unnatural events:

A lioness hath whelped in the streets,
And graves have yawned, and yielded
  up their dead.
Fierce fiery warriors fight upon the
  clouds,
In ranks and squadrons and right form
  of war
Which drizzled blood upon the Capitol.
The noise of battle hurtled in the air,
Horses did neigh, and dying men did
  groan,
And ghosts did shriek and squeal about
  the streets.   (2.2.18–25)

. . . The lioness is Wrath, and from her loins will spring forth "ranks and squadrons and right form of war," while the ghost of Caesar appears solemnly in the streets. We have not yet heard the dream; Shakespeare leaves it for Caesar himself to recount . . . to Decius.

She dreamt tonight she saw my statue,
Which like a fountain with an hundred
  spouts
Did run pure blood, and many lusty
  Romans
Came smiling, and did bathe their hands
  in it.
And these does she apply, for warnings,
  and portents,
And evils imminent. And on her knee
Hath begged, that I will stay at home
  today.   (2.2.81–87)

. . . Decius begins immediately to discredit Calpurnia's prediction. He commences with what is by now a familiar note: "This dream is all amiss interpreted," and offers instead his own "interpretation":

It was a vision, fair and fortunate.
Your statue spouting blood in many
  pipes,
In which so many smiling Romans
  bathed,

Signifies, that from you great Rome
  shall suck
Reviving blood, and that great men shall
  press
For tinctures, stains, relics and
  cognizance.
This by Calpurnia's dream is signified.
          (2.2.89–95)

It is the dissimulator now who cries, "thou hast misconstrued everything." He takes the manifest content of Calpurnia's dream and attributes to it a clever if wholly fabricated set of latent thoughts, which are the more impressive for their psychological insight. Caesar is flattered, as Decius had predicted, and resolves to go to the Capitol. His last doubts are abruptly erased when Decius suggests that he will be offered a crown and warns that refusal to go will seem

          a mock
Apt to be rendered, for someone to say,
"Break up the Senate till another time,
When Caesar's wife shall meet with
  better dreams."   (2.2.101–104)

This is a thrust well calculated to strike home. But there is a curious ambiguity about Calpurnia's dream, and the real irony of the situation is that Decius' spurious interpretation of it is as true in its way as Calpurnia's. . . .

For all its richness, however, the scene of Calpurnia's dream is rivaled in significance by a much more tangential scene, which seems at first glance oddly out of place in the plot. The scene of Cinna the poet is in many ways the most symbolically instructive of the whole play: it demonstrates in action the same theme of misinterpretation with which we have been so much concerned. Cinna the poet, a character unrelated to his namesake Cinna the conspirator, appears only in this scene,

Related Readings

which may be seen as a kind of emblem for the entire meaning of *Julius Caesar*. We encounter him as he makes his way along a Roman street, and his opening lines describe his dream:

> *I dreamt tonight, that I did feast with*
> *   Caesar,*
> *And things unluckily charge my fantasy.*
> *I have no will to wander forth of doors,*
> *Yet something leads me forth.*
>
> (3.3.1–4)

To "feast with Caesar" here means to share his fate—we may remember Brutus' "Let's carve him as a dish fit for the gods" (2.1.180). Cinna admits that he has had a premonition of danger, but that he has chosen to disregard it; "something"— misconstruction again—leads him forth. He is set on by a group of plebeians, their emotions raised to fever pitch by Antony's oration, and they rapidly catechize him on his identity and purpose.

> **THIRD PLEBEIAN:** *Your name sir, truly.*
> **CINNA:** *Truly, my name is Cinna.*
> **FIRST PLEBEIAN:** *Tear him to pieces!*
> *   He's a conspirator.*
> **CINNA:** *I am Cinna the poet, I am*
> *   Cinna the poet.*
> **FOURTH PLEBEIAN:** *Tear him for his*
> *   bad verses, tear him for his bad*
> *   verses.*

> **CINNA:** *I am not Cinna the conspirator.*
> **FOURTH PLEBEIAN:** *It is no matter, his*
> *   name's Cinna. Pluck but his name*
> *   out of his heart, and turn him going.*
>
> (3.3.26–34)

The scene is a perfect illustration of Cicero's verdict: "Men may construe things after their fashion, / Clean from the purpose of the things themselves." The taking of the name for the man—a thematically important element throughout this play, where Caesar is at once a private man and a public title—is symbolic of the overt confusion manifest in much of the action. Cinna's dream is a legitimate cause for anxiety, which he chooses to ignore at peril to himself. . . . The warning is given and ignored; the plebeians do not care that they attack the wrong man. In one short scene of less than 40 lines the whole myth of the play is concisely expressed.

Julius Caesar is a complex and ambiguous play. . . . The significance attached to the theme of "thou hast misconstrued everything" clearly depends to a large extent upon the reading—or misreading— of the play's many dreams. Here, . . . Shakespeare again demonstrates the great symbolic power which resides in the dream, together with its remarkable capacity for elucidating aspects of the play which otherwise remain in shadow. ■

What does Garber mean when she claims that the cry "thou hast misconstrued everything" could serve as an epigraph of the whole play?

Using words, magazine graphics, or original artwork, create a collage in which you illustrate some of the major arguments and themes presented in this selection.

Shakespeare Trivia: CAESAR *and* LINCOLN

by Norrie Epstein

Abraham Lincoln was known to be an avid fan of Shakespeare. The coincidences surrounding Lincoln's assassination are of Shakespearean proportions.

April 14, 1865: President Lincoln is assassinated by John Wilkes Booth, a member of one of the most famous acting families of the day. His father, Junius Brutus Booth, was named after Brutus, the assassin who killed Julius Caesar. On November 25, 1864, all three Booths had taken part in a benefit performance of *Julius Caesar,* John Wilkes's favorite play, to raise money for a statue of Shakespeare in Central Park in New York. Four months later, at a performance of *Our American Cousin,* John Wilkes, an ardent secessionist, shot and killed President Lincoln. In a final dramatic gesture, he leaped from the presidential box onto the stage screaming *"Sic Semper Tyrannis"* ("Thus Be It Ever to Tyrants," the motto of the state of Virginia).

Research Lincoln's fascination with Shakespeare. Compile at least five facts regarding his interest in the Bard.

Books featuring trivia lists have become quite popular. In groups, compile a series of trivia lists relating to the life and times of Julius Caesar or to the play itself. Be creative.

by Linda Burson

Spotlight *on* Brutus
The Prologue

Drama, to be truly appreciated, must be acted out and not just read. After all, "The play's the thing." Get ready to perform!

•   •   •

Actors are standing full back to the audience: Male 1 on the highest platform. Females 1 and 2 at center, Males 3 and 4 up left center, Males 2 and 5 down left. Lights and music cross fade to background level. Each actor turns full front on his/her line.

MALE 1: You all have heard how,

MALE 2: Once in ancient Rome,

FEMALE 1: When March stood at the mid-point,

MALE 3: At the Ides,

MALE 4: Conspiracy overpowered civic calm,

FEMALE 2: And Julius Caesar,

MALE 5: Praised and triumphed then,

FEMALE 2: Fell dead,

MALE 3: Dispraised,

FEMALE 1: Defeated at the hands of men who feared his strength.

ALL: In this our play,

MALE 2: We turn the light of Shakespeare on one man,

MALE 1: The honored Brutus,

MALE 5: weakened by the whispers,

FEMALE 1: taunts,

MALE 3: and flatteries

MALE 4: of men conspiring all around him.

FEMALE 2: Our focus shows how Brutus,

MALE 5: good but vulnerable,

MALE 1: gives way before these fawning men

MALE 2: and finds his dagger thrust in Caesar's side,

MALE 5: Killing the very man he loves.

FEMALE 2: 'Tis not the dagger's thrust that brings him down at last,

WOMEN: but his own conscience,

MEN: visualized as Caesar's ghost.

FEMALE 1: And then,

MALE 5: like Caesar,

FEMALE 2: he must die,

MALE 1: impaled on his own sword . . .

MEN: The lights go up. *[Lights up to full.]*

WOMEN: Listen:

ALL: To the recurring conspiracy.

In groups of four to seven, prepare a live or videotaped performance of "The Prologue." As part of your presentation, include a "spotlight" on another major character in the play.

RINSE THE BLOOD OFF MY TOGA

by Johnny Wayne and Frank Shuster

This classic television sketch is loosely based on Shakespeare's tragedy Julius Caesar. *Stand aside, Sherlock Holmes, and make room for ace Roman detective Flavius Maximus.*

The Dramatis Personae

FLAVIUS MAXIMUS	CASCA
BRUTUS	TREBONIUS
CALPURNIA	LIGARIUS
MARC ANTHONY	METELLUS CIMBER
CASSIUS	CINNA
CICERO	DECIUS

ANNOUNCER: This play is presented with apologies to William Shakespeare . . . and Sir Francis Bacon just in case.
[Fade video announcement as two soldiers turn to camera and do a take. Cut to pillar with sign on it . . . reading . . .
                    FLAVIUS MAXIMUS
                    Private Roman eye
Camera moves past pillar and we see Flavius at desk.]

FLAVIUS: Hi. My name is Flavius Maximus. I'm a private Roman eye.
[He rises and goes to wall holding a plaque with his number.]
    My license number is IXIVLLCCDIXMV. It also comes in handy as an eye-chart. If you can't read it you need glasses. . .
    Tonight, I'd like to tell you about the Julius Caesar Caper.
[Indicates bust of Julius Caesar.]
    It all began during the Ides of March. Right after the Festival of Pan . . . the god of theatrical criticism. I had just wrapped up the case of Suetonius the Gladiator . . . He'd been fixing fights at the Colosseum. He had a crooked lion that kept taking a dive. Anyway, this morning my secretary walks in . . .
[Cut to secretary staggering in carrying three heavy slabs.]

149

SECRETARY: Good morning, Flavius . . . here's the mail.

FLAVIUS: Nothing but bills. Anything else?

SECRETARY: Yeah . . . some guy outside wants to see you. He's awful excited about something.

FLAVIUS: O.K. Show him in . . .

SECRETARY: This way, sir.

BRUTUS: *[Enters nervously.]* Thank you.

BRUTUS: Are you Flavius Maximus, Private Roman eye?

FLAVIUS: Yeah, what's on your mind?

BRUTUS: Just a minute, are we alone?

FLAVIUS: Yeah, we're alone.

BRUTUS: You sure we're alone?

FLAVIUS: Yeah, I'm sure we're alone.

BRUTUS: Are you positive we're alone?

FLAVIUS: I'm positive we're alone.

BRUTUS: Well, who's that standing beside you?

FLAVIUS: That's you.

BRUTUS: Yeah . . . but can I be trusted?

FLAVIUS: I could see I was dealing with no ordinary man. This guy was a yo-yo. What's on your mind . . . ?

BRUTUS: Flavius Maximus, a terrible thing has happened. It's the greatest crime in the history of Rome.

FLAVIUS: All right, give it to me straight, what's up?

BRUTUS: Julius Caesar has been murdered.

FLAVIUS: Julius Caesar murdered? I couldn't believe my ears . . . Big Julie was dead.

BRUTUS: Yeah, he was killed just twenty minutes ago. It happened in the Senate. He was stabbed.

FLAVIUS: Stabbed?

BRUTUS: Right in the rotunda.

FLAVIUS: That's a painful spot. I had a sliver there once. So somebody snuffed Caesar . . . [Goes thoughtfully to table and pours drink from amphora.]

BRUTUS: I tell you all of Rome is in an uproar . . . and I came to you because you're the town's top private investigator. You got to find the killer.

FLAVIUS: I'll try.

BRUTUS: You can do it. You're the guy that nailed Nero.

FLAVIUS: That was just arson. This is murder one.

BRUTUS: Well, what do you say, Flavius? Will you take the case?

FLAVIUS: Wait a minute . . . not so fast . . . I'd like to know who I'm working for. Just who are you?

BRUTUS: I'm a Senator. I was Caesar's best friend. My name is Brutus.

FLAVIUS: Brutus, eh? O.K. Brutus, you got yourself a boy, I'll take the case.

BRUTUS: Great . . . now I don't want to embarrass you by talking about money.

FLAVIUS: Go ahead, embarrass me. My fee is a hundred denarii a day plus expenses.

BRUTUS: A hundred? I'll give you fifty.

FLAVIUS: A hundred.

BRUTUS: Fifty.

FLAVIUS: A hundred.

BRUTUS: All right, seventy-five.

FLAVIUS: O.K., seventy-five.

BRUTUS: Done. Now, my chariot is outside . . . let's go.

FLAVIUS: Wait a minute . . . whoa . . . payable in advance . . .

BRUTUS: O.K. [Drops coins on table.] There you are.

FLAVIUS: And here's your receipt . . . [Hammers away on slab with chisel.] Received from Brutus 75 denarii. [Hands it to Brutus.]

BRUTUS: You chisel pretty good.

FLAVIUS: Not as good as you. Let's go. [They exit.

Cut to chariot driving through the Via Appia.]

FLAVIUS: We made our way to the scene of the crime through the Via Appia. The street was crowded with the usual characters, slaves, legionnaires, gladiators, courtesans, and sneaky little men who came out of doorways and offered you postcards from Gaul. Before long we found ourselves at the Senate.

[Cut to Senate scene. Senators milling around in a turmoil of anxiety. Enter Flavius and Brutus.]

151

BRUTUS: Well, this is where the murder took place.

FLAVIUS: You mean Big Julie was wasted right here?

BRUTUS: Right.

FLAVIUS: Well, where's the corpus delicti?

BRUTUS: The what?

FLAVIUS: The corpus delicti. Don't you understand plain Latin? Corpus, corporus—corporum—masculine body.

BRUTUS: Oh, the stiff. Over here.

[Brutus leads him over to the body with nine knives in it.]

FLAVIUS: Break it up, you guys. [Kneels.] Holy Zeus . . . nine daggers. . . .

BRUTUS: Whoever did this should be charged with willful homicide.

FLAVIUS: And practising acupuncture without a licence.

BRUTUS: Well, have you got any ideas?

FLAVIUS: First of all, I gotta make a positive identification.

BRUTUS: What do you mean?

FLAVIUS: Is this really Julius Caesar? Have you got a coin on you?

[Brutus, puzzled, hands Flavius a coin. Flavius studies coin and body.]

FLAVIUS: Yeah, that's him.

BRUTUS: [Takes coin . . . looks at it.] Doesn't look like him.

FLAVIUS: That's tails.

BRUTUS: All right, Flavius, get moving.

FLAVIUS: All right, fill me in on the set-up. Who are those shifty-looking characters over there?

[Cuts to group, then back.]

BRUTUS: Shifty-looking? Those are Senators.

FLAVIUS: That explains it.

BRUTUS: They were all here when it happened. [Cut to individual faces . . . very sinister . . . as Brutus calls their names.] That's Casca . . . Trebonius, Ligarius, Metellus Cimber . . . Decius Brutus, Cinna . . .

FLAVIUS: Cinna the Poet?

BRUTUS: No, the other one.

FLAVIUS: That's good. The poet's nothing. Virgil he ain't . . . "Arma virumque cane" . . . that's poetry? By the way, who's the guy with the lean and hungry look?

[Cut to Cassius.]

BRUTUS: That's Cassius.

FLAVIUS: Such dudes are dangerous. Looks like he died twelve years ago and came back for his galoshes. Who do you think is the likeliest suspect?

BRUTUS: That fellow next to him.

[Pan over . . . it is Brutus. Then pan to Flavius.]

FLAVIUS: Wait a minute! That's you.

BRUTUS: I know. But can I be trusted?

[Camera zooms in to Flavius.]

FLAVIUS: This case was taking on a new interesting flavour . . . bananas. All right, you guys . . . Somebody in this joint knocked off Big Julie and you're all suspects!

CAST: [Ad libs, protest.]

FLAVIUS: You can all go . . . but don't leave Rome.

[They exit grumbling and Calpurnia passes them, looks sadly at the body and places a lily on it. Cut to Flavius and Brutus.]

FLAVIUS: Who's the woman?

BRUTUS: That's Caesar's wife. Her name is Calpurnia.

FLAVIUS: Well, she's a suspect. [Walks to Calpurnia.] Pardon me . . . Mrs. Caesar.

CALPURNIA: Yes?

FLAVIUS: [Shows badge.] Flavius Maximus, Private Roman eye. I'd like to ask you a few questions. What do you know about this?

CALPURNIA: I told him! I told him, Julie, don't go! Julie, don't go. I told him. But no, he wouldn't listen.

FLAVIUS: Now, look Mrs. Caesar . . .

CALPURNIA: I pleaded with him, Julie don't go. If I told him once I told him a thousand times. Julie! Don't go.

FLAVIUS: Mrs. Caesar . . .

CALPURNIA: But would he listen to his own wife? It's like talking to a wall. I said . . . Beware, it's the Ides of March already. But he wouldn't listen.

FLAVIUS: All right, take it easy. Sergeant, would you take Mrs. Caesar home?

SERGEANT: Come along, Ma'am.

CALPURNIA: I told him, Julie, don't go. Don't go to the Forum . . . a funny thing will happen . . . I told him, Julie, don't go.

FLAVIUS: I don't blame him for going.

BRUTUS: [Joins him.] Well, what do you think?

FLAVIUS: I don't know. This is a real puzzler. Not a clue.

[They sit on the steps.]

BRUTUS: Cheer up, Flavius. You'll come up with the right answer. After all, Rome wasn't built in a day.

FLAVIUS: What was that?

BRUTUS: Rome wasn't built in a day.

FLAVIUS: Say, that's pretty good. Rome wasn't built in a day. I'd like to use that sometime.

BRUTUS: You really like it?

FLAVIUS: Yeah.

BRUTUS: It's yours.

FLAVIUS: Thanks. Now, let's reconstruct the crime . . . where was

Caesar when it happened . . . ?

BRUTUS: He was heading for the Senate when all of a sudden . . .

FLAVIUS: Right. And . . . just a minute . . . There's somebody behind that pillar . . . *[Draws dagger.]* . . . Freeze!

[Marc Anthony comes out. He is carrying a sack.]

FLAVIUS: Come on out, you . . . up against the pillar . . . spread 'em. *[He frisks him . . . He's clean.]*

FLAVIUS: All right, buddy, what are you hanging around for?

MARC: Why shouldn't I? I'm Marc Anthony. . . .

FLAVIUS: All right, so you're Marc Anthony. I still want to know what you're doing here.

MARC: I just delivered the funeral oration over the body of Caesar. I said "Friends . . . Romans . . . countrymen . . . lend me your ears."

FLAVIUS: Yeah? What have you got in the sack?

MARC: Ears.

FLAVIUS: Get out of here . . .

MARC: Wait a minute . . . don't you want to know who knocked off Caesar?

FLAVIUS: Yeah. You know who did it? What's his name?

MARC: His name is . . . ah-ee-ah-oh-oo . . . *[He falls dead with dagger in back.]*

FLAVIUS: That's an interesting name. Must be from out of town.

BRUTUS: No, look. He's dead.

FLAVIUS: What a confusing case. All I've got for clues are two dead bodies and a sack full of ears . . .

BRUTUS: Now look, Flavius, I'm paying you 75 denarii a day. Let's have some action.

FLAVIUS: All right . . . don't get your toga in a knot. I got a pal. Cicero. He runs a little club in the Via Flaminia. He should have a few answers.

BRUTUS: That's the idea. Get out among the people. Ask questions. Circulate. When in Rome do as the Romans do . . .

FLAVIUS: What was that?

BRUTUS: When in Rome do as the Romans do.

FLAVIUS: Hmm. That's very good.

BRUTUS: You like it?

FLAVIUS: Yeah.

BRUTUS: It's yours.

FLAVIUS: Thanks. Well . . . I'll head down to Cicero's. See you later.

BRUTUS: Ave Atque Vale.

FLAVIUS: Ciaou baby.

[Dissolve to Cicero's club. It is a flashing neon-type sign that reads: Cicero's Swingles Club.]

FLAVIUS: Come Singular . . . Go home Plural.

[Cut to inside. Camera pans and then cuts to group.]

FLAVIUS: *[During camera action above.]* Cicero's is a hang-out where I can usually get a few answers. It's a small place with a few tables and a trio . . .

[Flavius comes in and walks to bandstand. Group sings "Hic . . . Haec . . . Hoc" song. Flavius goes to bar. Cicero is polishing a goblet.]

FLAVIUS: Hey, Cicero . . . what's shaking, baby?

CICERO: *[Turns.]* Hey, Flavius Maximus; long time no see. What's going down?

FLAVIUS: Nothin' much. What's new with you?

CICERO: Everything's cool. What are you drinking?

FLAVIUS: Gimme a Martinus.

CICERO: You mean a Martini.

FLAVIUS: If I want two, I'll ask for them.

[Cicero pours martini in goblet after shaking it.]

FLAVIUS: Look . . . I guess you heard somebody hit Julius Caesar.

CICERO: Yeah . . .

FLAVIUS: You know anything?

CICERO: Try that guy over there.

[Flavius walks toward man.]

FLAVIUS: Flavius Maximus . . . what do you know about the Caesar hit?

SCIPIO: Nothing much . . . except it wasn't done by an out-of-towner.

FLAVIUS: Local talent?

SCIPIO: Yeah . . .

FLAVIUS: How do you like that? Julius Caesar . . . Conqueror of Gaul, of Britain . . . of all the far-flung provinces . . . the greatest emperor we've ever had killed by a fellow Roman. Terrible.

SCIPIO: That's Ancient Rome, baby . . . you never know when they're gonna . . . do it to you.

[Camera pans to Flavius and zooms in. He shrugs and starts to walk on. Longer shot as:]

FLAVIUS: The whole caper was beginning to make sense. It was a Roman who had put out the contract on Big Julie. Probably one of those Senators . . . but which one? As I stood there trying to make sense out of it all, a strange exotic perfume, a familiar scent I recalled from the scene of the crime . . . *[Goes to woman with back to camera.]* . . . All right, sister, start talking . . .

CALPURNIA: *[Turns.]* I told him, Julie, don't go . . . I said don't go, Julie, don't go . . .

[Flavius sees her to the door.]

FLAVIUS: You know, I'm beginning to think it was suicide.

[Cut to Cicero.]

CICERO: Look, Flavius . . . I think I know who you're looking for.

FLAVIUS: You mean which Senator killed Caesar?

CICERO: No . . . it wasn't one Senator . . . they all did it.

FLAVIUS: Yeah . . . nine senators . . . nine daggers. But who set it up? Who put out the contract?

CICERO: You mean Mr. Big?

FLAVIUS: Yeah . . . what's his name?

CICERO: His name is . . . Aaaaahahahahahaa . . .

FLAVIUS: Right, and what's his address . . . Cicero . . . Cicero . . .

[Takes out hourgass and holds Cicero's pulse.]

FLAVIUS: I would never do any more martinus jokes with him. He was deader than Pompeii.

FLAVIUS: This was shaping up bigger than I thought. Suddenly I sensed somebody beside me . . . *[Flavius rises, revealing Brutus.]*

BRUTUS: Hello, Flavius.

FLAVIUS: Brutus, what are you doing here?

BRUTUS: I was looking for you. Who's that on the table?

FLAVIUS: Cicero . . .

BRUTUS: That's a funny place for him to carry a knife. In his back.

FLAVIUS: He was stabbed through the portico.

BRUTUS: That's even more painful than the rotunda.

FLAVIUS: Et tu, Brute?

BRUTUS: Well, have you come up with an answer? Who killed Julius Caesar?

[Camera moves in on Flavius.]

FLAVIUS: Slowly the pieces fell into place. I put two and two together and it came out I-V. I think I know who did it.

BRUTUS: You do?

FLAVIUS: You see, the clue to the murder was the way it was done . . . the modus operandi.

BRUTUS: The what?

FLAVIUS: Modus operandi . . . don't you understand plain Latin? The method used to kill him. The Gimmick.

BRUTUS: Oh, gimmick I know.

FLAVIUS: Greek he understands. He's probably one of those guys who says et cetera.

BRUTUS: Well, who did it?

FLAVIUS: It's obvious . . . you see there were nine daggers in Caesar . . . and there were nine senators . . . ergo . . .

BRUTUS: Ergo?

FLAVIUS: Don't start up. They were all in on it. But somebody was the ringleader. Now, which one . . . who was around for all the hits? Not only Caesar, but Marc Anthony . . . *[Crosses to body.]* . . . and the bartender . . . only one of them, Brutus, or should I say . . . Mr. Big?

BRUTUS: What are you getting at?

FLAVIUS: If the sandal fits, wear it. You put out the contract on Big Julie.

BRUTUS: You're out of your head. I hired you to find the killer.

FLAVIUS: Pretty smart, but not smart enough. All right, do I get a confession or do I have to call in a couple of centurions to lean on you?

BRUTUS: All right, shamus. I did it. I admit. I killed Caesar . . .

FLAVIUS: But why?

BRUTUS: Why? Because he was crazy . . . crazy, I tell you. He wanted to rule the world. He thought he was another Napoleon.

FLAVIUS: Napoleon! This is 44 B.C. Napoleon hasn't been born.

BRUTUS: I told you he was crazy.

FLAVIUS: Forget it! Come on, I'll call a chariot and we'll go downtown.

BRUTUS: Not so fast. *[Pulls out dagger and holds it to Flavius' throat.]* I'm getting out of here. And don't try to follow me unless you want to wind up in the bottom of the Tiber in a cement toga.

FLAVIUS: I can't believe it's Brutus talking. Brutus . . . the noblest Roman of them all. Perhaps the wisest man in our whole history.

BRUTUS: I wouldn't say that.

FLAVIUS: Neither would I, but you've got the dagger up my nose.

BRUTUS: Well, don't try to stop me. . . .

[Cut to Brutus lashing horse in chariot set, intercutting to same chariot set with Flavius to simulate chase . . . maybe different coloured chariots.]

FLAVIUS: Although Brutus had a head start on me, I knew where he was heading . . . the scene of the crime . . . the Senate . . .

[Cut to Senate steps. Brutus runs in and darts into temple-like edifice. Sounds of siren, hoofbeats to stop, and horse whinny. Flavius runs in followed by two tribunes and a crowd gathers.]

FLAVIUS: All right, you centurions. Let's have a little crowd control . . . Keep those people back . . . and hand me that horn.

[Tribune gives him large ram's horn-type bullhorn.]

FLAVIUS: *[P.A. amplification.]* All right, Brutus . . . This is Flavius Maximus. It's the man talking. I know you're in there. Come on out!

BRUTUS: Come and get me.

FLAVIUS: Now listen . . . you haven't got a chance. I've got the Senate surrounded. Throw down your sword and come out with your hands up.

BRUTUS: Come and get me.

FLAVIUS: Get smart, Brutus . . . we can smoke you out . . .

BRUTUS: I'd like to see you try, Flatfoot.

FLAVIUS: All right, get me the incense.

BRUTUS: Incense?

[Sound of crash of glass. Crowd Shots. Cut to Brutus coughing as he comes out of a smoke-filled temple.]

FLAVIUS: *[Grabs Brutus and holds a dagger to him.]* Freeze . . . one false move and I'll fill you full of bronze.

[Two tribunes come and grab his arms.]

BRUTUS: You got me. But I'll be back.

FLAVIUS: I don't think so. This isn't a series. All right, read him his rights . . . cuff him . . . and book him.

BRUTUS: I'll be back. Just remember . . . all roads lead to Rome.

[He starts to exit with tribunes, but Flavius goes after him and stops him.]

FLAVIUS: Hey, what was that one?

BRUTUS: All roads lead to Rome.

FLAVIUS: Hey, that's the best. All roads lead to Rome.

BRUTUS: You like it?

FLAVIUS: Yeah . . .

BRUTUS: Well, you can't have it.

SENATOR: Good work, Flavius. All Rome salutes you. Hail Flavius.

CROWD: Hail Flavius.

FLAVIUS: Thank you. And now, if you'll excuse me, I have a note from an unknown admirer inviting me out to dinner. You sure your husband won't mind . . . ?

CALPURNIA: Frankly, I don't care. I told him, Julie don't go. Don't go Julie, I said . . . but would he listen . . . ?

FLAVIUS: *[Puts up his hand.]* You know you have the right to remain silent.

CALPURNIA: Nevertheless . . . I told him Julie don't go . . .

ॐ ॐ ॐ

What different stereotypes does this script poke fun at?

If you were William Shakespeare, what would you say to the writers of this particular sketch? Respond in whatever form you wish, for example, a dialogue, a poem, a letter of complaint or one of praise.

REVIEWERS

The publishers and editors would like to thank the following educators for contributing their valuable expertise to the development of the *Global Shakespeare Series*:

Nancy B. Alford
Sir John A. Macdonald High School
Hubley, Nova Scotia

Philip V. Allingham, Ph.D.
Golden Secondary School
Golden, British Columbia

Francine Artichuk
Riverview Senior High
Riverview, New Brunswick

Carol Brown
Walter Murray Collegiate Institute
Saskatoon, Saskatchewan

Rod Brown
Wellington Secondary School
Nanaimo, British Columbia

Brian Dietrich
Queen Elizabeth Senior Secondary
Surrey, British Columbia

Alison Douglas
McNally High School
Edmonton, Alberta

Kimberley A. Driscoll
Adam Scott Collegiate
Peterborough, Ontario

Burton Eikleberry
Grants Pass High School
Grants Pass, Oregon

Gloria Evans
Lakewood Junior Secondary School
Prince George, British Columbia

Professor Averil Gardner
Memorial University
St. John's, Newfoundland

Joyce L. Halsey
Lee's Summit North High School
Lee's Summit, Missouri

Carol Innazzo
St. Bernard's College
West Essendon, Victoria, Australia

Winston Jackson
Belmont Secondary School
Victoria, British Columbia

Marion Jenkins
Glenlyon-Norfolk School
Victoria, British Columbia

Sharon Johnston, Ph.D.
Boone High School
Orlando, Florida

Jean Jonkers
William J. Dean Technical High School
Holyoke, Massachusetts

Beverly Joyce
Brockton High School
Brockton, Massachusetts

Judy Kayse
Huntsville High School
Huntsville, Texas

Doreen Kennedy
Vancouver Technical Secondary School
Burnaby, British Columbia

Betty King
District 3
Corner Brook, Newfoundland

Ed Metcalfe
Fleetwood Park Secondary School
Surrey, British Columbia

Janine Modestow
William J. Dean Technical High School
Holyoke, Massachusetts

Mary Mullen
Morell Regional High School
Morell, Prince Edward Island

Steve Naylor
Salmon Arm Senior Secondary School
Salmon Arm, British Columbia

Kathleen Oakes
Implay City Senior High School
Romeo, Michigan

Carla O'Brien
Lakewood Junior Secondary School
Prince George, British Columbia

Bruce L. Pagni
Waukegan High School
Waukegan, Illinois

Larry Peters
Lisgar Collegiate
Ottawa, Ontario

Margaret Poetschke
Lisgar Collegiate
Ottawa, Ontario

Jeff Purse
Walter Murray Collegiate Institute
Saskatoon, Saskatchewan

Grant Shaw
Elmwood High School
Winnipeg, Manitoba

Debarah Shoultz
Columbus North High School
Columbus, Indiana

Tim Turner
Kiona-Benton High School
Benton City, Washington

James Walsh
Vernon Township High School
Vernon, New Jersey

Kimberly Weisner
Merritt Island High School
Merritt Island, Florida

Edward R. Wholey
Sir John A. Macdonald High School
Halifax, Nova Scotia

Garry Williamson
Murdoch Mackay Collegiate
Winnipeg, Manitoba

Beverley Winny
Adam Scott Secondary School
Peterborough, Ontario

About the Series Editors

Dom Saliani, Senior Editor of the *Global Shakespeare Series*, is the Curriculum Leader of English at Sir Winston Churchill High School in Calgary, Alberta. He has been an English teacher for over 25 years and has published a number of poetry and literature anthologies.

Chris Ferguson is currently employed as a Special Trainer by the Southwest Educational Development Laboratory in Austin, Texas. Formerly the Department Head of English at Burnet High School in Burnet, Texas, she has taught English, drama, and speech communications for over 15 years.

Dr. Tim Scott is an English teacher at Melbourne Grammar School in Victoria, Australia, where he directs a Shakespeare production every year. He wrote his Ph.D. thesis on Elizabethan drama.

ACKNOWLEDGMENTS

Permission to reprint copyrighted material is gratefully acknowledged. Every reasonable effort has been made to contact copyright holders. Any information that enables the publisher to rectify any error or omission will be welcomed. Selections may retain original spellings, punctuation, and usage.

Historical Background to Julius Caesar by Isaac Asimov slightly adapted from ASIMOV'S GUIDE TO SHAKESPEARE VOLUME I by Isaac Asimov. Copyright © 1970 by Isaac Asimov. Used by permission of Doubleday, a division of Bantam Doubleday Dell Publishing Group, Inc. *The Ides of March* by C.P. Cavafy, translated by Rae Dalven from THE COMPLETE POEMS OF CAVAFY by C.P. Cavafy, copyright © 1961 and renewed 1989 by Rae Dalven, reprinted by permission of Harcourt Brace & Company, the estate of C.P. Cavafy, and Chatto and Windus. *The Fall of Rome* by Susan L. Gilbert which appeared in NEW VOICES IN AMERICAN POETRY, copyright © 1989, published by Vantage Press. *Calpurnia and Portia* by Dr. Sarojini Shintri from *Woman In Shakespeare* which appeared in RESEARCH PUBLI-CATION SERIES 32, Karnatak University, Dharwad, 1977. *I Saw Caesar Pass in Splendour* by Richard Woollatt. Reprinted by permission of the author. *How to Report on What You've Seen or Read* by Frank Barone. Copyright © 1986 by The National Council of Teachers of English. Reprinted with permission. *The Killing of Julius Caesar "Localized"* by Mark Twain from SKETCHES NEW AND OLD, published by Penguin USA. Public domain. *A Conversation of Three* by G.W.F. Hegel from CLIO, Volume 7, Number 2, Winter 1978. Reprinted with permission. *Freedom, Farewell!* by Phyllis Bentley. Copyright © 1936. Reprinted by permission of the Peters, Fraser & Dunlop Group Ltd. *The Bitterness of Love* by Dana K. Haight. Copyright © 1993 by The National Council of Teachers of English. Reprinted with permission. *Bugbears by Moonlight* by H.N. Hudson, 1872. Public domain. *Dream and Interpretation: Julius Caesar* by Marjorie B. Garber from DREAM IN SHAKESPEARE: FROM METAPHOR TO METAMORPHOSIS by Marjorie B. Garber, copyright © 1974 by Yale University. Reprinted by permission of Yale University Press. *Shakespeare Trivia: Caesar and Lincoln* by Norrie Epstein from THE FRIENDLY SHAKESPEARE by Norrie Epstein. Copyright © 1993 by Norrie Epstein, Jon Winokur, and Reid Boates. Used by permission of Viking Penguin, a division of Penguin Books USA Inc. *Spotlight on Brutus: The Prologue* by Linda Burson from PLAY WITH SHAKESPEARE by Linda Burson, New Plays Incorporated, Charlottesville, VA 22905. Copyright © 1992. Reprinted with permission. *Rinse the Blood Off My Toga* by Johnny Wayne and Frank Shuster. Copyright © 1955. Reprinted with permission of Frank Shuster and the estate of Johnny Wayne.

ARTWORK

Yuan Lee: cover, 12, 22–23, 34, 46–47, 52–53, 56, 68–69, 78, 90–91, 94, 108–109; **Folger Shakespeare Library,** reprinted with permission: first page of *Julius Caesar* from the First Folio (1623), 7; earthquake from *Prodigiorum* (1557), 26; Pompey's theatre from *Roma* (1694), 30; augurer from *Prodigiorum* (1557), 41; bayed hart from *The Noble Art of Venerie* (1611), 62; "I had rather be a dog, and bay the moon" from *A Choice of Emblemes* (1586), 83; **John James:** a performance at the Globe Theatre from *Shakespeare's Theatre* (Simon and Schuster, 1994), 8; **Mike Reagan:** 10; **Nicholas Vitacco:** 11, 123; **IGNITION Design and Communications:** series logo; marginal art: 13, 19, 23, 30, 42, 85, 97, 103; **Wesley Lowe:** 116–119; **Paul Morin:** 121; **Pierre-Paul Pariseau:** 125; **Bruce Roberts:** 129; **Carmelo Blandino:** 131; **Alain Massicotte:** 136; **Andrew Peycha:** 142; **Thom Sevalrud:** 144; **Russ Willms:** 150, 157.